German Military Vehicles in the Spanish Civil War

German Military Vehicles in the Spanish Civil War

A Comprehensive Study of the Deployment of German Military Vehicles on the Eve of WW2

José María Mata, Lucas Molina and José María Manrique

Collection José Manuel Campesino

Translated by Steve Turpin White

FRONTLINE BOOKS

GERMAN MILITARY VEHICLES IN THE SPANISH CIVIL WAR
The Deployment of German Armour and Vehicles on the Eve of WW2

José María Mata, Lucas Molina and José María Manrique
Translated by Steve Turpin White

Original Spanish language edition entitled Vehículos Alemanes en la Guerra Civil Española published by Galland Editorial Books in 2015.

This English edition first published in 2020 by Frontline Books,
an imprint of Pen & Sword Books Ltd,
Yorkshire – Philadelphia.

ISBN: 978-1-47387-883-9

CIP data records for this title are available from the British Library.

Printed and bound by TJ International Ltd, Padstow, Cornwall.

Pen & Sword Books Ltd incorporates the Imprints of Aviation, Atlas, Family History, Fiction, Maritime, Military, Discovery, Politics, History, Archaeology, Select, Wharncliffe Local History, Wharncliffe True Crime, Military Classics, Wharncliffe Transport, Leo Cooper, The Praetorian Press, Remember When, Seaforth Publishing and Frontline Publishing.

For more information on our books please email us at info@frontline-books.com, write to us at the above address, or visit:
www.frontline-books.com

Contents

Introduction

Between 1936 and 1939 Spain witnessed and participated in a bloody civil war. The international circumstances prevailing at the time were responsible for the major involvement of three countries in the Spanish conflict: Hitler's Nazi Germany, Mussolini's fascist Italy, and Stalin's communist Soviet Union.

Apart from men and all kinds of weapons, the foreign contingents also sent vehicles, either for transport (motorcycles, cars, trucks and buses) or actual combat (tanks and armoured cars). They also sent support vehicles for towing and powering artillery pieces, searchlights and the like, for maintenance tasks (mobile workshops, water bowsers and refuelling vehicles), for telecommunications services (mobile listening, radio and telephone stations), and for the recovery of broken down or unserviceable materiel (crane trucks and trailers).

Vehicles and trailers from all kinds of sources and in all sorts of condition began to arrive in Spain and were distributed around its towns and cities. The result was a geographically scattered hotchpotch of the most modern and up-to-date commercial products from top European automotive makes (Mercedes-Benz, Krupp, Daimler, Maybach, Lancia, Fiat, Ansaldo, etc.) and also from other lesser known, but of no lesser quality, Russian manufacturers that were beginning to emerge as a result of the famous five-year plans of the Stalinist economy.

In this book we will be making a detailed, in-depth examination of the various vehicles produced by German vehicle manufacturers of the day (many of which are still in business today) which the German armed forces sent to Spain as part of their aid to the rebel forces. These vehicles formed part of the various units of the Condor Legion and Franco's army, providing the Nationalists with mobility and firepower while supplying the German army with a test bench for their equipment. The Germans would learn a great deal about these vehicles' strengths and weaknesses, which would stand them in good stead for the world war that was just around the corner.

While the wide range of models, makes and purposes of the German vehicles used in the Spanish Civil War is undoubtedly an incentive to any researcher, that same enormous variety makes it hard to be certain that the list is complete. However, we can assure that all the vehicles featured in this book did, in one way or another, take part in the Spanish war 1936–39. The authors encourage you, our readers, to point out to us any errors or omissions that you may find in the following pages; we are open to any improvements or additions that you may wish to suggest to us.

We hope you will enjoy this book with its scores of photos, drawings and data tables, and immerse yourself in the fascinating world of military vehicles.

José María Mata, Lucas Molina and José María Manrique

Chapter 1

Rebellion in Spain and German Support

The failure of the civil-military coup in a number of the *divisiones orgánicas* or territorial divisions into which Spain was divided on 18 July 1936, turned what should have been a lightning rebellion into a long and bloody civil war. Initially there was little coordination, either among the rebels or among the Republican authorities. It was not until the first few days had passed that the two sides became clearly defined; until then, neither side's commanders had any real capability of directing operations in their zones.

Once the battle lines had become clear after those early days of uncertainty, the only units equipped with any armoured vehicles (it would be an exaggeration to call them tanks) in the Spanish army at the time were divided up evenly. The unit stationed in Madrid was in government hands while the one based in Zaragoza was in Nationalist occupied territory. Both had archaic and obsolete Renault FT-17s armed with a 7mm machine-gun, which had been acquired in the early 1920s for the Rif War. There were just half a dozen tanks on each side (plus a few Schneider CA-1s and Trubia A-4s); a pitiful total by any reckoning and certainly insufficient for modern warfare. Unsurprisingly, Nationalists and Republicans would soon look for ways to strengthen their meagre tank forces.

Early in September 1936 a significant event occurred, one which did not involve any of the rebel army commanders, but which brought about a substantial change in the military situation of the Nationalist forces in the conflict. This event has received little attention in the extensive bibliography on the Spanish Civil War, but it was fundamental to the subsequent unfolding of events and, in particular, to the arrival of German aid to the rebels.

While it is true that German aid, recently assured by the Reich's decision to support the military uprising against the Popular Front,

San Fernando Airfield, 21 September 1936. Franco and a number of members of the *Junta de Defensa Nacional* who were summoned to meet to decide who would have sole command of operations having just disembarked from a military DC 2. Among them can be seen Mola, Cabanellas, Orgaz, Dávila, Gil Yuste, Queipo and Franco (with his back to the camera). In the foreground, the commander of *La Legión, Teniente Coronel* Juan Yagüe. (*GB*)

had already started to arrive in Spain as part of Operation *Magic Fire*, the arrival in Spain of *Oberstleutnant* Walter Warlimont as head of the German Military Mission to Nationalist Spain would mark an important turning point in the provision of material aid to the rebels.

On 25 August, *Generaloberst* Werner von Blomberg, commander of the German armed forces (*Wehrmacht*), summoned a then young and obscure artillery officer named Walter Warlimont to his office in Berlin. There the commander-in-chief of the armed forces told him that Hitler

Before 18 July 1936, there were two tank regiments in Spain, although between them they could muster no more than a dozen armoured vehicles, all relics from of First World War and the Moroccan campaign. Nevertheless, some of them saw action in the Civil War, such as these two belonging to 2nd Tank Regiment of Zaragoza. The photo was taken in 1938. (*JMMD*)

had taken the decision to provide more support to Franco, and that Italy would follow suit. The amount of German support would be limited due to the conditions restricting Germany's rearming. Some war materiel would be sent, but German personnel would only be sent there to train Spanish troops in the handling of the unfamiliar German weapons.

Generals Franco (with garrison cap) and Queipo de Llano (with peaked cap) together in Sevilla. They were the leaders of the uprising in the south of Spain. (*GB*)

Generaloberst von Blomberg was appointed Minister of Defence by Hindenburg in 1933. In 1936 he would be promoted to *Generalfeldmarschall*, the first in the Nationalist-Socialist period. Two years later he would fall into disgrace after his marriage to a woman with a murky past. (*GB*)

WALTER WARLIMONT

Born in Osnabrück (Germany) on 3 October 1894. Although his father was a publisher, Walter preferred to pursue a career in the armed forces. He entered the Artillery Academy and began to serve in the German army in June 1914. During the First World War he fought on the Western Front as a battery commander, where he earned a number of field promotions.

Once the war was over, Warlimont joined one of the new Freikorps formations before transferring to the new Reichwehr. In 1922, while serving with the General Staff, he was sent to England in 1926 to learn English, and then to the USA in 1929 to continue with his studies. As an army *Oberstleutnant* he was sent to Spain in September 1936, where for a brief period he acted as the 'Representative of the *Wehrmacht* before Franco' or, to put it another way, Military Attaché in Nationalist Spain.

Warlimont was not only a soldier but was also well-versed in economics and politics which, in August 1936, qualified him to take up the post of Director of the Economics Department of the *Heereswaffenamt*, the German army's weapons agency. His colleagues there considered Warlimont to be a competent officer with a firm and unwavering character, and it was precisely his performance in that department which led von Blomberg to place him in charge of the mission in Spain, the purpose of which, in the words of Abendroth, was 'to safeguard German interests in the economic arena'.

He was the right man at the right time; he was an officer with the appropriate training to allow him to act as an intermediary between Nationalist Spain and the all-powerful German army; between Franco and the German Staff. He also benefited from an unusual advantage in that he was well-respected and moved comfortably in the social and political circles of the Third Reich.

After a short stay in Spain, Warlimont returned to Germany in November 1936 after a number of issues with Berlin. A month and half later he took command of the 26th Artillery regiment, based in Düsseldorf.

In September 1938, Warlimont was transferred to the *Oberkommando der Heer* (OKH or Supreme Command of the Army) where he became *Generalmajor* Alfred Jodl's right hand man. As such he took part in most General Staff conferences and the preparation of many operational plans and war directives. He was one of the officers seriously injured in the assassination attempt on Hitler in July 1944, and as a result he was forced to retire from active service in September of that same year. In May 1945 he was arrested and put on trial in Nüremberg where he was sentenced to eighteen years in prison, of which he served eleven. On leaving prison in 1957

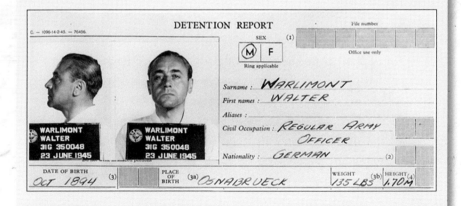

he wrote a book of memoires entitled *Inside Hitler's Headquarters 1939–45*, in which he made an exhaustive analysis of the day-to-day life in Hitler's headquarters during the turbulent years of the Second World War. Walter Warlimont died in the city of Kreuth (Upper Bavaria) on 9 October 1976.

Wilhelm Canaris wearing the uniform of *Kapitän zur See* of the German navy. It was at this time that he began to serve in the *Abwehr*. The fact that he spoke Spanish facilitated his relations with the authorities of Nationalist Spain. (*GB*)

Generale Mario Roatta, Warlimont's Italian opposite number. He would be the first commander of the Italian contingent in the Spanish war. (GB)

Warlimont's mission would be to act as Germany's representative to Franco, to look after the interests of his fellow Germans in Spain, and to ensure that Germany's military support of Spain was rewarded by a supply of raw materials.

On 26 August, Walter Warlimont had a meeting with Wilhelm Canaris, head of the German Secret Service (*Abwehr*) and a man who was knowledgeable about Spanish affairs. In their meeting they prepared for their imminent trip to Rome, where they would be meeting *Generale* Mario Roatta in order to continue working closely with the Italians on the matter of sending military materiel to Spain. Immediately afterwards, Warlimont returned to Berlin to have a meeting with *Generalleutnant* Helmuth Wilberg, head of the recently created *Sonderstab W*, a special staff whose mission was to coordinate German participation in the Spanish war.

Warlimont's duties were specified in an annex to the document he was given prior to his departure for Spain. In essence, his role was to examine all possible ways of supporting the rebels, to advise the Spanish High Command, to safeguard German interests in politico-military and economic matters, and to cooperate with the representatives of the Italian forces in Spain.

The day after receiving his instructions, Warlimont left once again for Rome for another meeting with Roatta and from there they travelled together to the Port of Gaeta. There they boarded a torpedo boat belonging to the Italian navy which took them Tangiers. The following day they made the short journey to Tetuán where they boarded a Junkers Ju 52 to fly to Sevilla. On landing they were met by their initial opposite number in Nationalist Spain, *General* Gonzalo Queipo de Llano, who had joined the uprising in Sevilla and commanded the Army of the South.

General Queipo de Llano in one of his famous radio talks broadcast by Radio Sevilla. (*VT*)

On 6 September, they were met in Cáceres by *General* Francisco Franco, who had set up his headquarters in this city in the southern region of Extremadura. Roatta introduced Warlimont to Franco, who presented Warlimont with the orders that he had been sent by the German officer's superior, von Blomberg.

On arrival, Warlimont relieved *Oberst* Alexander von Scheele with immediate effect and established his centre of operations in the Hotel Cristina in Sevilla. From there he made countless tours of the territory in rebel hands in order to analyse

Werner von Blomberg was the commander of the German armed forces in 1936. He had fought in the First World War, earning the famous *Pour le Mérite* medal which hangs at his neck. (*GB*)

The Hotel Cristina in Sevilla was the centre of operations of the German representatives von Schelle and Warlimont. (*JMCB*)

Wilhelm Canaris was head of the *Abwehr*, the German secret service. He informed Hitler of Franco's assumption of leadership at the Burgos Military Junta. (*GB*)

One of the founders of the company HISMA Ltda was the German citizen, Johannes Bernhardt, who took advantage of the opportunity provided by the Spanish war to convince the German authorities to side with the rebels. This company played an important role in the development of the war, acting first as a channel and later as a clearing house for most Hispano-German transactions during the Civil War. (*GB*)

ongoing operations and send reports back to Berlin. Since Germany did not officially have either weapons or men involved in the Spanish war, Walter Warlimont used two aliases during the time he was in Spain, 'Guido' and 'Woltersdorff'.

On 12 September, Warlimont sent his first report on Nationalist forces' movements during the first months of the war and on the use the Spanish were making of the materiel provided by Germany up to that point. The *Oberstleutnant*'s report confirmed Franco's leadership of the Military Junta at Burgos, a matter on which Hitler had already been reliably informed by two sources; firstly, by Canaris, Head of the *Abwehr*, and secondly by Bernhardt, director and joint founder of the company HISMA Ltda.

On the subject of how the war was progressing, Warlimont made mention of the good service the aircraft supplied by the *Luftwaffe* had provided in the initial phases of the fighting and in the ferrying of the rebel troops from Africa to Spain across the Strait of Gibraltar. However, the German *Oberstleutnant* was sceptical regarding the future of military operations in Spain because 'reserves were running out'. It was his opinion that the war could only be won quickly if Germany stepped up its supply of material aid; in particular, armoured cars or tanks, and anti-aircraft and anti-tank guns, weapons of which the Spanish had almost none.

Warlimont asked Berlin to send an armoured force, together with anti-tank materiel. He was pleasantly surprised by the response from Berlin, since what he received far exceeded his expectations.

Wilhelm Ritter von Thoma in the uniform of the *Afrika Korps*. He had been a theoretician of armoured units since the twenties. He played an essential role in the organization of Nationalist army tanker troops in Spain. (*BA*)

German High Command approved the dispatch of a battalion-strength armoured force, complete with a staff unit, two tank companies, a transport company, a workshop company, an anti-tank training unit, and an armoury unit. The then *Oberstleutnant* von Thoma, a pioneer of German tank units, was chosen to lead the force.

Thus on 23 September, *Oberstleutnant* Wilhelm Josef Ritter von Thoma, commander of the 2nd Battalion of *4./Panzer-Regiment* based in Schweinfurt, was posted to Spain. His mission was to take command of the German armoured group which would be embarking for Spain in a week's time.

Wilhelm Josef Ritter Von Thoma

Born on 11 September 1891 in Dachau, von Thoma's leaning towards a military career led him to enlist in the Bavarian army, in which he was promoted to infantry *leutnant* on 2 August 1914 in the 3rd Regiment.

Leutnant Wilhelm Thoma was sent to the front where he was wounded during the Somme offensive but refused to be evacuated in order to stay with his troops. On 12 October 1915, he received a chest wound during the Serbia campaign and was hospitalized. In February 1916 he returned to the front, fighting in the Verdun-Bois d'Avocourt sector.

On 5 July 1916, the 11th Bavarian Infantry Division was posted to the Ugli-Gruziatyn area to cover the Austrian withdrawal after the Russian offensive at Brusilov. For his actions that day *Leutnant* Thoma was awarded the highest award for bravery in combat, the Knight's Cross of the Bavarian Military Max Joseph Order, and was given the title of *Ritter* (Knight). In 1917 he took part in several operations in the Alsace area, specifically in the battles of Aisne and Champagne, in the autumn battles in Flanders (Belgium), and in operations in the area of the rivers Meuse and Moselle. In January 1918 he was promoted to *Oberleutnant*.

In April 1918 he was wounded once again, in the First Battle of Kemmel (Belgium), and again refused to be evacuated. After the last of *General* Ludendorff's offensives in the summer of 1918 he was taken prisoner by the Americans. On being released fifteen months later, he returned to Germany in 1920 and joined the new *Reichwehr*.

After attending various courses and holding several posts related to vehicles, in April 1934 von Thoma was promoted to *major* and given the task of organizing the *Kraftfahr-Lehrkommando* (Motorized Instruction Command) at Ohrdruf (Thuringia). This was the first German tank unit to be created since the end of the First World War.

Together with *General* Lutz and *Generalmajor* Heinz Guderian, Von Thoma was a pioneer of the development and formation of German armoured forces. On 15 October 1935, *Major* von Thoma was made commander of the 2nd Battalion of *4./Panzer-Regiment*, based in Schweinfurt, part of *2. Panzer-Division*, commanded by *Generalmajor* Heinz Guderian.

On 1 August 1936, von Thoma was promoted to *Oberstleutnant* and a month and a half later, on 23 September 1936, he became a *z.b.V.* (special forces) officer, serving in Spain until 31 May 1939 as commander of the *Panzer* contingent of the German *Wehrmacht* known as *Panzergruppe Drohne*.

On his return to Germany on 31 May 1939, now with the rank of *Oberst*, he was attached to the Staff of the *3./Panzer-Regiment*. Between 19 September 1939 and 5 March 1940, he commanded *3./Panzer-Regiment*, before being transferred to *Oberkommando der Heer* (Army High Command). There he was appointed to a post of a higher rank as head of motorized troops, a post he held until 17

July 1941, when he was given provisional command of *17.Panzer-Division*, a unit which took part in Operation *Barbarossa*.

In October 1941 he was given command of *20.Panzer Division* stationed on the Russian front. Late in December 1941 von Thoma was awarded the Knight's Cross of the Iron Cross.

At the end of June 1942 von Thoma relinquished command of *20.Panzer Division* and returned to OKH as an inspector of motorized troops. A little later, on 1 August, he was promoted to the rank of *Generalleutnant*.

On 1 September 1942, he was made commander of the armoured units of the *Afrika Korps*, and two months later he was promoted to *General der Panzertruppe (Generaloberst)*. He was captured at Tel el Mampsra by British troops during the Second Battle of El Alamein.

Wilhelm Ritter von Thoma died in Dachau, the town of his birth, on 30 April 1948, shortly after his fifty-seventh birthday.

A number of photographs depicting training in Germany before 1936, showing the armoured vehicles most commonly used at that time, the *Panzerkampfwagen I Ausf A* and *Ausf B*. Despite being light and only lightly armoured, they were a good vehicle for training tank crews. Their worth as a tank in which to do battle with equivalent enemy tanks, however, left much to be desired. (*JMCB*)

Grafenwöhr 1935

Chapter 2

Panzergruppe Drohne

Coat of arms of the city of Neuruppin where *6.Panzer-Regiment* was based. On the right we can see the regimental insignia which decorated a plate belonging to the tableware of *6.Panzer-Regiment*. (*GB*)

On 20 September 1936, all the officers, NCOs and men of the two battalions making up *6./Panzer-Regiment* were assembled at the base at Neuruppin, where their commanders called for volunteers for a mission abroad of some importance, without at any time telling them that the mission was to be undertaken on Spanish soil. What they *were* told was that this would not be a mere exercise or manoeuvres; they would be coming under live fire and might be taken prisoner by the enemy, wounded, or even killed on the battlefield.

Nearly all the men took a step forward and volunteered for the secret mission abroad; a romantic adventure far from the fatherland for some, and for most a good opportunity to put into practice the skills and tactics learned over so many months. None of them knew their destination nor the scope or difficulty of the mission, but all of them understood that it would be no walk in the park.

Parade of the first *Panzertruppen* in Berlin. On the left of the photo, Chancellor Adolf Hitler with the commanders of the German armed forces. (*JMCB*)

A German ornamental saucer of the period, representing the first armoured units of the German army. Notice that they are communicating with one another by semaphore flags. (*JMCB*)

Instruction in Germany with *Panzerkampfwagen I Ausf A* tanks. They were fitted with a Krupp M305 engine producing 57hp at 2,500rpm, giving a top speed of 37kph and a range of 150km. In the photo below, we can clearly see inside the turret the Zeiss RFZ2 gun sight (also called the Heiden scope) with a magnification of 2.5. Track throwing was a frequent problem with these light tanks. (*LMF*)

Two photographs taken during the voyage of the steamer *Girgenti* en route to Sevilla. This was one of the vessels that carried the German ground forces to Spain in September 1936. (*JMCB*)

Once the men were chosen,* they were initially organized into one staff unit, two tank companies, one transport company and one workshop company. All units were full strength and the tankers were equipped with 41 *Panzerkampfwagen I Ausf. A* tanks, which was the regulation type for the unit at the time, as well as various models of other vehicles, trucks and motorcycles, and all the weapons needed to complete the mission.

The first volunteers, 267 men, were transported to Döberitz, near Berlin, where they drew extra pay for their most immediate expenses, such as civilian clothing. While away from Germany they would, in theory, temporarily cease to belong to the *Wehrmacht* as it was necessary to maintain the pretence that German military personnel were neither fighting alongside nor supporting one of the sides in the Spanish war.

COMMANDER					
COMMAND STAFF					
1st PANZER COMPANY	2nd PANZER COMPANY	ANTI-TANK COMPANY	TRANSPORT COMPANY	WORKSHOP COMPANY	ARMOURY
VEHICLES & EQUIPMENT	41 x PANZER I			11 x LIGHT CARS	
	10 x BÜSSING NAG 650 TRUCKS			24 x PAK 35/36 GUNS	
	6 x WORKSHOP TRUCKS			19 x TANK TRANSPORTER TRAILERS	
	45 x CARGO TRUCKS			18 x MOTORCYCLES	

The German tankers, kitted out with civilian clothes and false passports, formed an odd group of young, curiously regimented German travellers, as they waited to set off, ostensibly to spend their summer holidays at an as yet unknown destination under the hot sun of a country that none of them knew anything about. The group was transported by road to the port of Stettin where they were to embark, fully convinced that their final destination was Danzig (a Polish administered city, once part of the German Empire and now reclaimed by the National-Socialist Reich from the Polish state).

On 28 September 1936, the members of the Panzer unit boarded the merchant ships *Passages* and *Girgenti*, which would also be carrying all

---

* The lowest rank selected was *gefreiter*, equivalent to the Spanish rank of *cabo* (lance corporal); once in Spain all were promoted to the equivalent of *sargento (feldwebel)*.

the equipment and materiel they would need to carry out their mission in Spain.

On 7 October 1936, *Passages* and *Girgenti* entered Spanish waters and from that point on were escorted by the pocket battleships *Admiral Scheer* and *Deutschland*, and the torpedo boat *See Adler*. Towards the end of the day they arrived at the port of Sevilla where the men disembarked, and their equipment was unloaded.

Although the men of the *Panzergruppe* were keen to enter into action, they were not sent to the front right away because their main mission was to teach Spanish soldiers how to drive the German tanks and use them in combat. For this purpose, the trainers would draw on the tactical lessons learned in Germany on how to wage modern armoured warfare. Shortly after its arrival in Sevilla, the *Panzergruppe* was sent by rail to Cáceres, leaving between 8 and 10 October.

The pocket battleship *Admiral Scheer*. This was one of the German warships that escorted the expedition bringing the two German armoured companies to Sevilla. (*JMCB*)

A picture taken on 9 October 1936. Unloading of *Panzerkampfwagen I* A tanks at the station of Aldea del Cano, a village close to the Arguijuelas castles, the destination of all the materiel sent from Sevilla. Clearly visible is the paintwork with which these tanks arrived in Spain, which was no different from that used by operational units Germany: Panzer grey with brown patches. As can be seen, these tanks were not fitted with either rear air filter shields or engine grilles. (*JMCB*)

The German registered steamer *Girgenti* arriving at the port of Sevilla, carrying the troops and tanks of the 2nd Tank Company commanded by *Oberleutnant* Wolf. (*JMCB*)

Two members of the *Gruppe Thoma* wearing the first version of this contingent's uniform, posing in front of a *Panzer I* camouflaged with branches and leaves, a recent arrival from Germany. (*JMCB*)

About a week later, on 18 October, they were reviewed by Franco at their base at the Las Arguijuelas castles. At the time *Oberstleutnant* von Thoma was commanding the unit with *Major* Eberhard von Ostman as second-in-command and Chief of Staff.

A little later, on 25 November, thirty-seven more men arrived at Sevilla on board the *Urania*. Together with some of their fellow tankers already in Spain and twenty-one new tanks, in this case *Panzerkampfwagen I Ausf. B* originally belonging to *4./*Panzer-Regiment, they formed the 3rd Tank Company of the *Panzergruppe* under the command of *Hauptmann* Karl Ernst Bothe.

Oberleutnant Heinz Wolf, commander of the 2nd Panzer Company of the "*Gruppe Thoma*". (*JMCB*)

On gate duty. On the left a Spanish soldier and on the right a German guard. (*JMCB*)

Cáceres

Aldea Moret

The entrance to Arguijuela de Arriba Castle. (*JMCB*)

Germans formed up in the courtyard of the Arguijuela de Arriba Castle, waiting for their orders. (*JMCB*)

The castle of Arguijuela de Abajo.

The castles of Arguijuela de Abajo and, in the background, Arguijuela de Arriba. (*JMCB*)

Two views of the conical tents erected at the
entrance to Arguijuela de Arriba Castle. (*JMCB*)

Arguijuela de Arriba.

Valdesalor

Castillo de
Arguijuela de Abajo

Castillo de
Arguijuela de Arriba

Aldea del
Cano

The full complement of the German
nd Panzer Company at Arguijuela
e Arriba Castle. (*JMCB*)

THE CASTLES

The Las Arguijuelas castles are two fortified
buildings in the province of Cáceres, some fourteen
kilometres to the southeast of the provincial capital.

The castle of Arguijuela de Abajo was built as
a fortified house towards the end of the fifteenth
century for Francisco de Ovando *El Viejo*. The
building was later added to during the first half of
the sixteenth century, when it gained its towers,
machicolations, turrets, loopholes and arrow-slits.
At the same time the living quarters were improved
and extended, and an interior patio was built with a
columned gallery.

The neighbouring castle of Arguijuela de Arriba,
was built on the top of a hill for Diego de Ovando de
Cáceres at the beginning of the sixteenth century. It
was the work of Pedro de Larrea, a master builder
of the Order of Alcántara, and features a spacious
interior patio from one side of which rises the main
structure with its columned ground floor gallery.
The family's coat of arms is carved over the main
gate. The castle is arranged around a central patio
with a tower at each corner, three of them round
and the fourth, attached to the keep, square.

Oberstleutnant Wilhelm von Thoma with his interpreter Klaus. In the background, *Alférez* Sanz Ruano. (*JMCB*)

Feldwebel Arnold Kasulke enjoys his breakfast. (*JMCB*)

The Germans arrived at grape harvest time. (*JMCB*)

Wolf and Willing with interpreter Kübler in an off-road vehicle. (*JMCB*)

The 2nd Panzer Company's field kitchen with some kitchen hands. (*JMCB*)

Oberleutnant Wolf and *Leutnant* Willing with a fellow German on a *Panzerbefehlswagen* I B. (*JMCB*)

Peeling potatoes for the field kitchen.

Several members
of *Panzergruppe
Drohne*, newcomers
to Spain, pose
behind the cabin of a
truck. (*JMCB*)

A visit by *Generalísimo* Franco, commander-in-chief
of the rebel forces, to the *Panzer-Gruppe* at the
Arguijuelas complex (Cáceres). (*JMCB*)

A practical machine gunnery class in which Spanish soldiers are being explained the weaponry carried by a *Panzer I*. Its machine guns could also be fitted with a bipod to be used off the vehicle. (*JMCB*)

Medal bar with German and
Spanish medals belonging to a
member of the Condor Legion.
(*JMCB*)

German soldiers clean and prepare the *Panzer I*'s 7.92 mm Dreyse machine guns and load
their magazines. (*JMCB*)

A moment of rest and relaxation. German soldiers listen to the radio, drink and smoke during an autumnal evening in Cáceres. (*JMCB*)

The Germans set up their tents in the gardens of Arguijuelas de Abajo Castle. In the photo a sentry stands next to a number of men at the entrance to one of these improvised dormitories. (*JMCB*)

The headquarters of the *Panzergruppe* soon moved to Cubas de la Sagra, a town in the province of Madrid, where the training centre and workshop were also set up.

By the end of 1936 a total of 307 men from the German army had arrived in Spain. By 31 December, the unit had lost eight men; two men died in accidents and the other six were sent back to Germany for various reasons.

PanzerGruppe Thoma in January 1937	
Group Commander	Oberst Wilhelm von Thoma (23/9/36-31/5/39)
Staff Unit	35 Men: 4 leutnants, 18 stabsfeldebels, 9 feldewbels & 1 interpreter
Chief of Staff	Oberstleutnant Eberhard von Ostman (8/10/36-29/8/37)
Doctor	Major Johannes Engelhardt (8/10/36-1/8/37)
Quartermaster	Major Fritz Muehlenkamp (8/10/36-15/5/37)
1st Tank Company	65 men: 7 leutnants, 43 stabsfeldwebels, 9 feldwebels, 1 medic & 2 interpreters
Company Commander	Major Joachim Ziegler (8/10/36-18/3/38)
Deputy Company Commander	Hauptmann Ferdinand von Planitz (8/10/36-28/9/37)
Section Commander	Oberleutnant Erwin Strauchmann (8/10/36-20/7/37)
2nd Tank Company	66 men: 7 leutnants, 44 stabsfeldwebels, 9 feldwebels, 1 medic & 2 interpreters
Company Commander	Major Heinz Wolf (8/10/36-25/7/37)
Deputy Company Commander	Hauptmann Gerhard Willing (8/10/36-14/9/37)
Section Commander	Oberleutnant Hannibald von Moerner (8/10/36-24/7/37) Killed at the front +
3rd Tank company	64 men (6-12-1936): 6 leutnants, 43 stabsfeldwebels, 9 feldwebels, 1 medic & 2 interpreters
Company Commander	Major Karl-Ernst Bothe (1/11/36-16/12/37)
Deputy Company Commander	Oberleutnant Karl Pfannkuche (1/11/36-6/12/37)
Section Commander	Oberleutnant Ottfried Sanfft von Pilsa (1/10/36-15/10/37)
Transport Company	36 men: 6 leutnants, 18 stabsfeldwebels, 9 feldwebels, 2 mechanics
Company Commander	Hauptmann Hans Schruefer (8/10/36-31/5/39)
Workshop	23 men: 1 leutnant, 8 stabsfeldwebels, 10 mechanics & 2 interpreters
Company Commander	Hauptmann Albert Schneider (1/11/36-31/5/39)
Head of Workshop	Leutnant Paul Jaskula (8/10/36-30/4/37) Died in plane crash
Anti-Tank Training Unit	9 men: 3 leutnants, 4 stabsfeldwebels & 1 interpreter
Unit Commander	Major Peter Jansa (1/11/36-18/3/38)
Armoury	6 men: 2 leutnants, 3 stabsfeldwebels & 1 armourer
Interpreters	2 group interpreters, attached to the Condor Legion
Total	307 Panzer-Gruppe men who arrived between September & December 1936

The ranks shown in the table are those held by the Germans stationed in Spain which were one rank higher than the ones they held in Germany. In brackets next to the names of the officers is the date of their arrival in Spain and the date of their departure or, when applicable, death.

Comandante José Pujales Carrasco and *Capitán* Juan García García talk to *Oberleutnant Wolf*, commander of the 2nd German Tank Company with the aid of interpreter Winkler. Behind Pujales stands *Teniente* Valsmoreno of the tank unit. (*JMCB*)

Spanish UNITS

The purpose of the presence in Spain of the recently formed *Panzergruppe Drohne* was to instruct and train Nationalist troops in the handling and battlefield use of the German *Panzerkampfwagen I* tanks, the special vehicles belonging to the transport and workshop units, and the various materiel supplied by the '*negrillos*' (the Spanish nickname at the time for both the Germans and their tanks), such as anti-tank guns, flamethrowers, etc.

A 37mm PaK 35/36 anti-tank gun. The Germans provided twenty-four guns like this in the first consignment of materiel. In the photo, master armourer Hanfler and *Feldwebel* Koch. (*JMCB*)

On 1 October, a tank battalion was created in Cáceres with personnel belonging to the 27th Infantry Regiment *Argel*. A week later it was sent to the Las Arguijuelas castles where on the 12th of the month the unit was placed under the command of retired *Comandante de Infantería* José Pujales Carrasco. He had formerly belonged to the Renault FT-17-equipped *Compañía de Carros Ligeros de Asalto* (Light Assault Tank Company), attached to the *Escuela Central de Tiro de Infantería* (Central Infantry Firing School), and so had experience in training men in the handling of armoured vehicles.

The Spanish organized their unit along the same lines as the German unit that had just arrived at Cáceres: a staff unit, two tank companies, transport and workshop units, and an anti-tank company. The 1st and 2nd tank companies were commanded by *Capitán* José García, formerly of the Spanish Legion, and *Capitán* Juan García, respectively.

On 1 December another German tank company arrived at Cubas enabling a third Spanish tank company to be formed under the command of *Capitán de Infantería* Gonzalo Díez de la Lastra Peralta.

'Negrillo' Tank Battalion in October 1936	
Battalion Commander	Comandante José Pujales Carrasco
Staff Unit	Capitán Gonzalo Díez de la Lastra Peralta Teniente Juan Barrenchegure Barganza
1st Company	Capitán José García Tenientes: Eladio Baldovín López, Maximiliano Galiana Castilla & José Losada Vera NCOs: Brigadas Segundo Calvo Castro, Santos Sánchez Rollán, & Francisco Álvarez Porto, & Sargento Virgilio Orea Clemens
2nd Company	Capitán Juan García Tenientes: Antonio López de Haro, José Cerdán Salas & Ramón Fernández García NCOs: Brigadas Antonio González, Joaquín Ainoza Soro, Alberto Mateos Molinero, & Antonio Tegel Abad, & Sargento Eloy Martín Serrano

Coat of arms of the *Regimiento de Infantería "Argel"
no. 27*. This was a garrison regiment in Cáceres, some
of whose members were used to form a tank battalion in
1936. (*GB*)

In this photo we can see *Comandante* Pujales Carrasco (with white overall and a black beret,
facing the camera) with his three company captains. On the right, and from right to left,
José García García (with *La Legión* side-cap), Juan García García (with overall and black
beret) and Gonzalo Díez de la Lastra (with leather jacket and garrison cap). In the middle
and to the rear, three *Gruppe Thoma* instructors. The photo may have been taken in early
1937. (*JMCB*)

On the right of the photo *Oberstleutnant* von Thoma stands next to *Teniente Coronel* Asensio Cabanillas, head of one of the columns that marched on Madrid from Sevilla, wearing a soft fez (*tarbuch de regulares*), jersey and belting. The rest are Legionnaires belonging to one of the *banderas* (battalions) making up the column. The photo was taken in Navalcarnero on October 28, 1936. (*JMCB*)

From left to right, *Leutnant* Willing, *Comandante* Pujales, *Oberleutnant* von Thoma, *General* Sperrle (Sander) and *Oberleutnant* Aldinger, commander of the first 88mm anti-aircraft battery to operate in Spain. The photo was taken in Derio (Vizcaya) in June 1937. (*JMCB*)

From left to right, *Alférez* Tegel, *Alférez* Ainoza, *Oberleutnant* Bothe, *Capitán* Losada, interpreter Drechsel, and *Leutnant* Willing at Orduña (Vizcaya campaign). (*JMCB*)

From left to right, *Comandante* Pujales, interpreter Winkler and *Oberleutnant* Wolf. The need to use interpreters did not prevent there being a good understanding between Germans and Spanish. (*JMCB*)

On 1 October 1937, a fourth Panzer I tank company was created at Casarrubuelos (officially the 5th Company, belonging to the 2nd Group), under the command of *Capitán de Infantería* Pedro Jiménez. It was equipped with sixteen new tanks of the thirty received from Germany on 1 September. According to the organizational structure of the 1st Tank Battalion, this company was called the 5th '*Negrillos*' Company, probably to differentiate it from units equipped with T-26B tanks, which were called '*Rusos*' (Russian).

In order to organize two new companies equipped with tanks fitted with cannon, on 14 October 1937, orders came from Franco's headquarters (hereinafter also referred to by the Spanish acronym CGG) instructing *General* Orgaz to prepare all the Renault and Trubia tanks captured in the north for dispatch to the south, once they had been repaired. During the Santander campaign the Nationalists captured a total of thirteen Renault tanks and three Trubia tanks (almost certainly Trubia–Naval tanks, also called '*Euzkadis*' in numerous publications), and two Trubia-Landesas (very possibly armoured cars based on Landesa tractors). All were sent by the recovery service to the Sevilla Artillery Factory to be rebuilt; of these at least ten were returned to serviceable status and sent to the 2nd Tank Regiment in Zaragoza.

Entry of Nationalist troops in Bilbao. In the photo, a *Panzerbefehlswagen I Ausf. B* command tank (in the foreground) is followed by a similar, type A line tank through the streets of Bilbao, cheered on by excited civilians. In the command tank we can see *Comandante* Pujales Carrasco, commander of the Spanish armoured, dressed in a beige overall, belting and beret. (*OGL*)

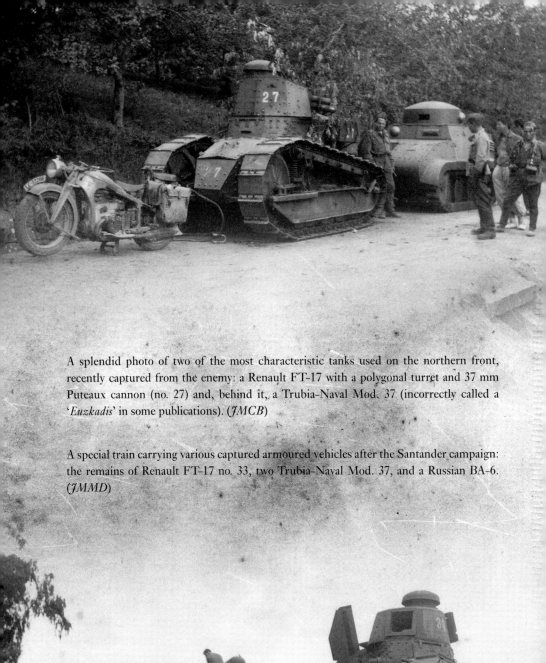

A splendid photo of two of the most characteristic tanks used on the northern front, recently captured from the enemy: a Renault FT-17 with a polygonal turret and 37 mm Puteaux cannon (no. 27) and, behind it, a Trubia–Naval Mod. 37 (incorrectly called a '*Euzkadis*' in some publications). (*JMCB*)

A special train carrying various captured armoured vehicles after the Santander campaign: the remains of Renault FT-17 no. 33, two Trubia–Naval Mod. 37, and a Russian BA-6. (*JMMD*)

Capitán Losada, commander of the 2nd Spanish Tank Company, poses for the camera with Leutnant Willing, second in command of the 2nd German Tank Company, at the northern front. (JMCB)

These tanks, together with ten more Renaults recovered in Asturias, were used to reinforce the Renault tank section which had been operating on the Aragón front under the command of Alférez de Infantería Alejandro Arruga.

In order to avoid confusion with the different rifle battalions that the 2nd Tank Regiment had been organizing during the campaign, in October 1937 the 'Negrillos' Tank Battalion was renamed the 1st Tank Battalion. On that same date the battalion's organizational structure was also modified. It would now comprise two tank groups each with three companies, two of Panzer I tanks and one of Russian T-26 tanks, in addition to other unattached units, as shown in the table below.

The 1st Tank Battalion in November 1936	
Battalion Command & Staff	Teniente Coronel José Pujales Carrasco
1st Group (formed on October 1)	Command and Staff: Comandante Gonzalo Díez de la Lastra Peralta 1st & 2nd Companies of "Negrillo" tanks. 3rd Company of "rusos" (Russian) tanks
2nd Group (formed on November 1)	Command and Staff: Comandante José García García 4th & 5th Companies of "Negrillo" tanks. 6th Company of Renault tanks (in the process of being replaced by Russian T-26 tanks)
Anti-Tank Company	
Transport Company	Capitán José Alfaro Páramo
	As from November 18 this unit was handed over to the Spanish. Due to the Increasing intensity of the war, the Germans began to fear becoming overly involved In ground operations and so they handed the unit over.
Workshop Company	Capitán Felix Verdeja Robles
	For the same reason as for the Transport Company, this unit was also handed over to the Spanish.

The Panzergruppe and Spanish units in 1938

After all the comings and goings of German personnel, by the end of 1937 *Panzergruppe Drohne* could muster just 124 men, of which only 103 actually served in the tank unit, the remaining twenty-one being assigned to the various infantry academies as instructors.

By then, four '*negrillo*' tank companies had already been formed in the Nationalist army, reducing the need for tank instructors. The previous year's total of 195 instructors had been whittled down to just thirty-five, whose mission was to maintain and support all the Spanish tank units fighting at the front. Similarly, the transport and workshop companies had been transferred to the Spanish army in November 1937; as in the case of the instructors, the German contingent was again significantly reduced as a result. Only ten *Panzergruppe Drohne* members remained in the transport company and only seven in the workshop company. The staff unit, anti-tank training unit, and the armoury continued with approximately the same number of men as in the previous year.

A cloth badge of one of the Navarre divisions. (*JMCB*)

A member of the *Panzergruppe* taking a photo with his Agfa camera.

A *Panzer I Ausf A* with a Spanish crew and a German instructor. (*GB*)

PanzerGruppe Drohne in January 1938	
Group Commander	Oberst Wilhelm von Thoma (23/9/36-31/5/39)
Staff Unit	33 men: Doctor, Quartermaster, 2 leutnants, 23 stabsfeldwebels, 5 feldwebels & 1 interpreter
Doctor	Hauptmann Hans Roessner (1/7/37-9/4/38)
Quartermaster	Hauptmann Max Franzbach (1/5/37-31/5/39)
Tank Company	35 men: 4 chiefs, 2 leutnant, 21 stabsfeldwebel, 2 feldwebels, 3 medics & 3 interpreters
Company Commander	Major Herbert Crohn (1/11/37-31/5/39)
Section Commanders	Oberleutnant H. Joachim Falkenberg von H. (1/11/37-2/5/38)
	Oberleutnant Axel von Levetzow (1/11/37-31-5-39)
	Oberleutnant Ernst Fremm (1/11/37-31/5/39)
Transport Company	10 men: chief, 1 leutnant, 5 stabsfeldwebels, 1 feldwebel & 2 mechanics
Company Commander	Hauptmann Hans Schruefer (8/10/36-31/5/39)
Workshop Company	7 men: chief, 5 stabsfeldwebel & 1 interpreter
Company Commander	Hauptmann Albert Schneider (1/11/36-31/5/39)
Anti-Tank Training Unit	8 men: chief, 2 leutnants, 3 stabsfeldwebels, 1 feldwebel & 1 interpreter
Unit Commander	Hauptmann Peter Jansa (1/11/36-18/3/38)
Armoury	6 men: 3 leutnants, 2 stabsfeldwebels & 1 armourer
Interpreters	3 interpreters, attached to the Condor Legion
Total	103 men

The Bilbao offensive. A number of Spanish and Italian soldiers near a German tank. The Italians were equipped with French-style Adrian helmets. (*JMCB*)

An excellent side view of a *Panzerbefehlswagen I Ausf B* in action. The Germans sent four of these armoured vehicles to the *Panzergruppe*. Behind can be seen two Russian T-26 tanks, captured by the Nationalists and used by their armoured units. (*FVB*)

Until February 1938 the tank unit continued to operate as the 1st Tank Battalion. However, in order to avoid the administrative problems created by the fact that its members had been drawn from so many different units, and to provide a monetary and prestige incentive by classifying the unit as a 'strike force', on 12 February Franco's headquarters issued Directive 4,745, whereby, for administrative purposes, all 1st Tank Battalion servicemen were attached to the Spanish Legion. Two weeks later the aforementioned battalion was assigned in its entirety to the *2º Tercio de la Legión* (Spanish Legion 2nd Regiment) and renamed *Bandera de Carros de Combate de La Legión* (hereinafter Spanish Legion Tank Regiment), with the organizational structure set out in the accompanying table.

Spanish Legion Tank Regiment in March 1938	
Regimental Command and Staff	Teniente Coronel José Pujales Carrasco
First Group	**Command and Staff:** Comandante Gonzalo Díez de la Lastra Peralta 1st & 2nd Companies of "Negrillo" tanks. 3rd Company of "rusos" (Russian) tanks
Second Group	**Command and Staff:** Comandante José García García 4th & 5th Companies of "Negrillo" tanks. 6th Company of "rusos" (Russian) tanks
7th Company (Renault)	At San Gregorio (Zaragoza). Obsolete materiel or materiel difficult to find spares for
Anti-Tank Company	37 mm PaK
Transport Company	Capitán José Alfaro Páramo
Workshop Company	Capitán Felix Verdeja Bardales
Tank School	Capitán La Cruz Lacacci (at Casarrubuelos, Madrid)
Depot Unit	

The *Cruz de Guerra* was awarded to many Germans at the end of the conflict. (*JMCB*)

Due to the ever-increasing size of the theatre of operations, on 1 October 1938, the units making up the tank regiment were beefed-up by giving them a second level of repair services and more servicemen. These groups became battalions and any Tank Regiment (*Bandera*) units not included in the groups continued with the same name and organizational structure, with the exception of the Workshop Company. This was considerably strengthened and often supported by the 'Vickers' mobile repair workshop headed by *Comandante de Artillería* Rubio. As a result of these changes, the Spanish Legion Tank Regiment changed its name to the Spanish Legion Tank Group (from *Bandera de Carros de la Legión* to *Agrupación de Carros de Combate de La Legión*), a name that remained unchanged until the end of the war.

The following table shows how it was organized.

Spanish Legion Tank Group in October 1938	
Group Command and Staff	Teniente Coronel (acting) Gonzalo Díez de la Lastra Peralta
First Battalion	**Command and Staff:** Comandante Maximiliano Galiana Castilla 1st & 2nd Companies of "Negrillo" tanks. 3rd Company of "rusos" (Russian) tanks. Repair workshop.
Second Battalion	**Command and Staff:** ComandanteJosé García García 4th & 5th Companies of "Negrillo" tanks. 6th Company of "rusos" (Russian) tanks. Repair workshop
Anti-Tank Company	Capitán Martín Ercilla García. Pak of 37 mm
Transport Company	Capitán José Alfaro Páramo
Workshop Company	Capitán Felix Verdeja Bardales
Renault Company	(Obsolete materiel or materiel difficult to find spares for)
Depot Unit	

Some Spanish soldiers of the *Bandera de Carros de Combate de La Legión* (Spanish Legion Tank Regiment), pose for the photo on a *Panzer I*. The guitar lends a touch of Spanish colour to the cold German steel. (*FVB*)

The FINAL months of PANZERGRUPPE Drohne

By early 1939 the headcount of von Thoma's German tank group had shrunk again. There were now fewer than 108 men serving in the staff unit, the tank company, the transport and workshop companies, the anti-tank training unit and the armoury.

Since their arrival in Spain in October 1936 until their departure in May 1939, von Thoma's men trained Spanish personnel in a variety of weapons and skills, including tanks, anti-tank guns, flamethrowers, mine launchers, anti-gas protection, and workshop and armoury skills.

A metal skull badge as worn on a tanker's black beret. (*JMCB*)

Formation of the *Agrupación de Carros de Combate de La Legión* (Spanish Legion Tank Group) in 1939. (*MSC*)

The two commanders of the German-Spanish tank unit in 1939: on the left, *Teniente Coronel* (acting) Gonzalo Díez de la Lastra Peralta; to the right, the then *Oberst* Wilhelm Ritter von Thoma. (*JMCB*)

PanzerGruppe Drohne in April 1939	
Group Commander	Oberst Wilhelm von Thoma (23/9/36-31/5/39)
Staff Unit:	39 men: Doctor, Quartermaster, 3 leutnants, 21 stabsfeldwebels, 12 feldwebels & 1 interpreter
Doctor	Major Hermann Essebruegge (1/3/38-31/5/39)
Quartermaster	Hauptmann Max Franzbach (1/5/37-31/5/39)
Tank Company	21 men: 3 chiefs, 2 leutnant, 11 stabsfeldwebel, 2 medics & 3 interpreters
Company Commander	Major Herbert Crohn (1/11/37-31/5/39)
Section Commanders	Oberleutnant Axel von Levetzow (1/11/37-31/5/39)
	Oberleutnant Ernst Fremm (1/11/37-31/5/39)
Transport Company	8 men: Chief, 4 stabsfeldwebels, 1 feldwebels & 2 mechanics
Company Commander	Hauptmann Hans Schruefer (8/10/36-31/5/39)
Workshop Company	7 men: Chief, 4 stabsfeldwebel, 1 feldwebel & 1 interpreter
Company Commander	Hauptmann Albert Schneider (1/11/36-31/5/39)
Anti-Tank Training Unit	7 men: 2 leutnant, 3 stabsfeldwebel, 1 feldwebel & 1 interpreter
Armoury	6 men: 3 leutnant, 2 stabsfeldwebel & 1 armourer
Infantry Instructors	19 men
Total	108 men

A German *leutnant* of the *Drohne* in service uniform. (*JMCB*)

In telegram No.1414 dated 20 April 1938, from Franco's headquarters in Burgos to *General* Orgaz, the head of the Mobilization, Training and Recovery bureau (MIR), Franco sent a summary of the training work carried out by von Thoma's group from 1 October 1936 to the end of March 1938.

Spanish personnel trained by the Panzer-Gruppe up to March 1938			
Type	**Officers**	**Sergeants**	**Privates**
German tanks	33	434 (of both categories)	
Type	**Officers**	**Sergeants**	**Privates**
Russian tanks	4	141 (of both categories)	
Spanish anti-tank guns	89	211	1.549
"Krupp Protze" (Kfz 69)		30 drivers	
Italian anti-tank guns	10	32	79
Flamethrowers	7	239 (of both categories)	
Tank transport on heavy trucks	1	75 drivers	
7.7 cm mine launchers	177	220	2.000
7.7 cm field guns	30	80	500
Anti-gas protection	180 officers, sergeants and privates*		
Workshops	1 master mechanic & 20 mechanics		
Tank and anti-tank gun master armourers	2 master armourers, 56 assistant master armourers		
Total number of men trained: 6,200			

*Also trained were the men of the 8th Regiment of the Spanish Legion and the Chemical Warfare Section of the Toledo Arsenal

The field commander of the Condor Legion, Wolfram von Richthofen, converses with *Oberst* Wilhelm Ritter von Thoma after the Condor Legion's air display held at Zaragoza. Behind them are Spanish officers and authorities who attended the event. (*GB*)

A poster of the organization 'Strength through Joy' (in German '*Kraft durch Freude*'), the owner of the two merchant ships that carried the Condor Legion back to Germany. (*JMCB*)

Once the Spanish war had ended, the remaining members of the *Panzergruppe Drohne* took part in the grand victory parade down the *Paseo de la Castellana* boulevard in Madrid on 19 May, and in the Condor Legion's official send-off presided by *Generalísimo* Franco on 22 May 1939, at the La Virgen del Camino airfield in León. From there they flew to Vigo where they were to board one of the ships chartered by the *Wehrmacht* to take them, the *Gruppe Imker*, and all their other fellow Condor Legionnaires back to Germany.

Two days later, on 24 May, five enormous German transatlantic vessels belonging to the organization *Kraft durch Freude* (Strength through Joy) arrived at Vigo loaded with medical supplies, surgical material, and food as a gift from the *Deutsche Arbeitsfront* (German Labour Front) to the Spanish state. These ships, the *Wilhelm Gustloff*, *Robert Ley*, *Stuttgart*, *Der Deutsche* and *Sierra Cordoba* took on board all the Germans still on Spanish soil and set sail for Hamburg on 26 May.

The 108 members of the *Panzergruppe Drohne*, together with the trainers of the various academies, the members of the *Gruppe Wolm* (radio-interception company), and the staff of the *Gruppe Imker*, boarded the *Sierra Cordoba*. This ship was fitted out to carry 900 passengers, although on this occasion it sailed with only 399 passengers on board.

Two German tankers on board the cruise ship *Sierra Córdoba*, which transported them back to their homeland in May 1939. (*JMCB*)

They arrived to a tremendous reception in Hamburg; they were greeted by *Reichsmarschall* Hermann Goering, together with Keitel and Raeder as heads of the *Heer* and of the *Kriegsmarine* respectively, on behalf of the *Führer*. Once they had disembarked, the troops marched past the dignitaries and the people of Hamburg. From there the Condor Legionnaires were taken to the army camp at Doberitz in the outskirts of Berlin to prepare for the grand parade of the unit as a whole, to be held the following week in the presence of Chancellor Hitler.

Before the parade in Berlin, on 3 June, *General* von Brauchitsch went to Doberitz to visit the army contingent of the Condor Legion (the tankers, instructors and members of the *Horch-Truppen*), whom he thanked enthusiastically for the services they had

Cruz de España (Spanish Cross) in bronze with swords. It was awarded to German combatants taking part in the Spanish Civil War. (*JMCB*)

rendered to the German Army 'in its struggle against Bolshevism in Spain'. He took the opportunity to decorate a number of men with the *Cruz de España* (Spanish Cross) in gold and silver.

In this ceremony a cuff title was awarded to commemorate and honour the German soldiers who fought in Spain between 1936 and 1939. It

Cuff title created to commemorate the presence of the German Army in the Spanish Civil War. (*JMCB*)

was awarded to members of the *Panzerlehr-Regiment, Nachrichten-Lehr-Abteilung* and *Versuchs-Abteilung*, the units which had provided the men who served in the *Gruppe Imker* as trainers and signals intelligence operatives during the three years the war lasted. This red, 32mm wide cuff title would be sewn around the soldier's left cuff and bore the legend *1936 Spanien 1939* in gold Gothic lettering.

At 10.00 hours on 6 June in Berlin, the grand victory parade of the Condor Legion commenced. More than 18,000 men, including the crews of the pocket battleships *Deutschland* and *Graff Spee*, formed up and marched past the foremost dignitaries of the German Reich and a strong representation of Spanish military top brass, led by generals Queipo de Llano, Solchaga, Aranda, García Valiño, and Yagüe.

Hitler welcomes the committee of Spanish generals who accompanied the Condor Legion on their return trip to Germany. From left to right: Queipo de Llano, Aranda, Solchaga, Yagüe and García Valiño. All of them, with the exception of Queipo de Llano, had just been awarded the *Gran Cruz de la Orden de la Águila Alemana*. (*LMF*)

Parade of the Condor Legion in Berlin on 6 June 1939. Two tankers of the *Panzergruppe Drohne* with black berets of a much larger size than were worn during the fighting. (*GB*)

Karl Kübler

Karl Kübler was a German citizen resident in Spain in 1936. At the very beginning of the Nationalist uprising of 18 July he volunteered to fight in Franco's army. On 23 September 1936, he was transferred to the *Gruppe Drohne* where he acted as an interpreter assigned to the *Panzergruppe* throughout the war.

Karl Kübler.

The courage and commitment he showed in the performance of his duties so impressed German High Command that he was given the rank of *Oberleutnant*, while the Spanish awarded him a campaign medal, the *Cruz de Guerra*, and the *Medalla Militar Individual*.

After the troops had been reviewed, all the Condor Legionnaires began to march in perfect formation under the arches of the Brandenburg Gate as far as the Lustgarten esplanade, where the main ceremony was to take place. There, from a grandstand erected for the occasion, Hitler and Goering addressed the troops, praising the courage of the German volunteers in the Spanish war. And so the Condor Legion passed into history.

Parade of the Condor Legion through the streets of Berlin. (*GB*)

Medal bar of a German combatant on which there hangs a variety of medals from the First World War, the Spanish Civil War, and the Second World War. (*JMCB*)

Chapter 3

German Tanks in Spain

Germany supplied the army contingent with a total of seventy-two tanks to be organized and put to use during 1936. They arrived in Spain in three separate consignments of forty-one, twenty-one and ten units respectively.

The first consignment received was the one which arrived on the vessels *Passages* and *Girgenti* together with the men and the rest of the materiel of the first two tank companies formed in October 1936. The tanks in question were forty-one *Panzerkampfwagen I*, which were used to form the first units of the Nationalist Army Tank Battalion.

A Panzer I Ausf. A belonging to the Nationalist Tank Battalion during the Bilbao offensive. (*GB*)

Operations of the Spanish legion Tank Group (October 1936 to April 1939)										
Theatre of operations	No. of engagements	Commanders		Officers		NCOs		Troops		Equipment losses
		W	D	HWW	M	H.-	M	H.-	M	
Madrid Front	183	-	-	13	3	14	3	91	22	36
Guadalajara	3	-	-	1	-	-	-	-	-	-
Bilbao	60	-	-	8	-	7	1	22	-	-
Brunete	17	-	-	1	-	4	-	11	-	1
Santander & Asturias	55	-	-	1	1	3	-	8	3	1
Aragón (Quinto, Belchite, Villamayor…)	14	-	-	-	1	-	-	2	1	1
Teruel	48	1	-	3	1	6	1	22	3	6
Aragón, Cataluña & Levante	292	-	-	28	5	43	8	152	23	26
Battle of the Ebro	111	1	-	32	6	48	5	170	24	28
Cataluña from Lérida to the French border	96	1	-	17	3	18	1	69	12	13
Madrid, Toledo and Guadalajara sectors	12	-	-	-	-	-	-	4	-	-
Andalucía: Peñarroya offensive	7	-	-	-	-	-	-	-	1	1
Total	904	3	-	104	20	143	19	551	89	125

Most of the German tanks sent to Spain were *Panzerkampfwagen 1 Ausf. A*, like those in the foreground of the photo. In the photo, we see the *Comandante Jefe* of the Spanish Tank Group 1st Battalion, Modesto Sáenz de Cabezón. (*FVB*)

When the tanks were assigned to the Spanish Legion (March 1938) they were adorned with the shield of the *Tercio*, as can be seen in the photo. (*GB*)

As we can see in the photo, the *Panzer I* arrived in Spain painted in German army colours. (*GB*)

During the Civil War, German tanks were identified in many ways. In this case we see tanks 'C' and 'P', displaying the relevant letters of the front plate and/or the glacis plate, together with Spanish flags, skulls, and code letters identifying the section to which the tank belonged. (*JMMD*)

Although the documentation to which the authors have had access does not specify the exact breakdown of those forty-one tanks, it is logical to suppose that among them there were at least three command tanks; one for the battalion, and the other two for each of the companies. The two full companies formed were organized on the basis of three sections of five tanks each, plus one for the company commander, making a total of thirty-three tanks (thirty line and three command). Of the eight remaining tanks of the forty-one received, one was of the type known as *Ohne Aufbau* in German (literally 'without bodywork').

These stripped-down tanks with no superstructure or turret would be used for the driver training courses at the Cubas de la Sagra school. The seven remaining tanks were used to cover the expected combat and operational losses and would later form part of a depot company. All the tanks received in this first consignment, except for the command tanks, were *Ausf. A* types, which in Spain were called Krupps after the engine they were fitted with.

The second contingent of German tanks, comprising twenty-one *Panzerkampfwagen I*, all probably *Ausf. B* type, reached Spain late in

Several *Panzer I* in the Vizcaya Campaign are about to be suitably camouflaged with tree branches. (*GB*)

Some of the *Panzer I* delivered to Spain were *Ausf. B* type tanks, with a longer chassis and a more powerful Maybach engine than the one used to power the *Ausf. A* type. (RA)

November 1936. In December, fifteen of these tanks, plus one command tank, were used to form the third company of the Nationalist army Tank Battalion at Cubas. Another five tanks were set aside to cover losses. Finally, the Condor Legion's accounts record a third consignment comprising ten *Panzerkampfwagen I* tanks, although neither the exact

The German tanks were handed over to the Spanish, who were trained how to handle them and taught modern armoured warfare tactics. (*JNP*)

date of their arrival nor the type of tanks delivered is known. We would hazard that the consignment could have been delivered early in 1937 to cover the large number of losses incurred by then.

A total of seventy-two tanks were sent to Spain via the Condor Legion.

Intensive battlefield use, the normal wear and tear suffered by complex, almost experimental, machinery, and losses incurred in the hard-fought Spanish war meant that these seventy-two tanks were not enough to keep the battalion operational. Therefore,

Emblem used by the armoured units of the Nationalist Army during the conflict.

the Spanish military authorities, which were tactically, operationally and organizationally responsible for the unit, decided to ask Germany for more *Panzers* 'if possible with a 20mm or larger cannon' in order to

A well-aimed anti-tank shell blew this *Panzer I* turret clean off its hull. (*GB*)

PANZERKAMPFWAGEN I AUSF. A

On 18 October 1936, Francisco Franco, recently named *Generalísimo*, carried out an inspection of the Tank Battalion at its base at the Arguijuelas Castles (Cáceres). In the sketch we see Franco facing Wilhelm von Thoma, commander of the German contingent, and a *Panzer I* tank in the original livery of the German army.

Medalla Militar Individual (Individual Military Medal).

Three photos in which we can see the inside of a *Panzer I*. The photo on the left shows the view from the driver's seat, with its levers, pedals, instruments and transmission, while the photos on the right are views from the side entry hatch, where we can see the tank commander's seat and the turret traverse wheel. (*GB*)

be able to engage on equal terms what was proving to be a very tough nut to crack on the battlefield; the Russian T-26, armed with a powerful 45mm cannon and two (in some cases three) 7.62mm machine guns.

The requests for more tanks were formally channelled through the company HISMA Ltda; the first on 13 July 1937 and the second on 12 November 1938. Franco was personally involved in the first request. He wrote to *General* Sander (Sperrle) asking him to try and speed up the process in Berlin, so that the thirty tanks and other materiel requested, including fifty 37mm PaK 35/36 anti-tank guns, could arrive sooner. The intervention of the head of the Condor Legion must have done the trick, since on 25 August, a German vessel, of whose name we are unaware, arrived at the Port of Vigo (although according to the documentation we have consulted the destination port should have been Ferrol) carrying eighteen *Panzerkampfwagen I Ausf. A* tanks. Five days later, on 30 August, the twelve remaining tanks, to complete the thirty, arrived at Sevilla. Both shipments were sent to Griñón and from there to Cubas, where a company of sixteen tanks was formed. The

A lieutenant of the Spanish Legion Tank Regiment poses in front of some German tanks. (*FVB*)

PANZERBEFEHLSWAGEN I AUSF. B (INITIAL VERSION)

The head of the *Panzergruppe Drohne*, Wilhelm von Thoma, with the second-in-command of the 2nd Company, *Oberleutnant* Gerhard Willing, in front of one of the command tanks sent to the contingent from Germany. It is a Panzer I type 'B' in command tank configuration. These vehicles remained in Spain at the end of the war.

Four photos of the *Panzerbefehlswagen I Ausf. B*, also called a command tank. The version received in Spain was the Ausf B type, although it was one of the first versions of the vehicle, without the ball mount for the machine gun or a raised turret for the tank commander. (*MSC above, and JMCB*)

remaining fourteen were used to bring the other companies back up to full strength after their combat losses.

In the second order, arranged through *Hauptmann* Wilhelmi, the German officer liaising between the *Gruppe Imker* and the CGG, thirty engines for the Panzers were requested, plus '20 German tanks, some armed with 20mm or larger calibre cannon'.

This request was also successful, so on 20 January 1939, *negrillo* tankers delivered the twenty tanks to the Tank Group, all of them *Panzer I Ausf. A* models fitted with Krupp engines. This was the last consignment of tanks to be sent to Spain from Germany during the 1936–39 Civil War. The final total was 122 *Panzerkampfwagen I* or *Panzerbefehlswagen I*, broken down as follows:

- 4 *Panzerbefehlswagen I Ausf. B*
- 21 *Panzerkampfwagen I Ausf. B*
- 96 *Panzerkampfwagen I Ausf. A*
- 1 *Panzerkampfwagen I Ausf. A (ohne aufbau)*[*]

By the beginning of 1937, the lightness of these tanks and their lack of firepower compared with their Russian counterparts equipped with 45mm cannon prompted the nationalists to consider fitting 20mm cannon to some of their tanks. After experimentally fitting Italian 20mm Breda cannon to a *Panzer I* and an Italian *Fiat-Ansaldo CV.33*, the German tank was seen to provide the best performance, and so one tank of each section was ordered to be modified to accept the 20mm cannon. The idea was to improve the offensive capability of the Nationalist armoured units, which were clearly inferior in both quantity and quality to their Republican counterparts.

Despite the order to fit ten *Panzer I Ausf. A* with cannon, in the end only four tanks were converted. A number of Russian T-26Bs captured from the Republicans and repaired in Sevilla made it less urgent to carry on with the conversions.

---

[*] This breakdown, provided by the authors and backed up by empirical and theoretical evidence regarding the tanks in Spain at the time, may contain errors, albeit none that are evidenced by any official document of the time.

PANZERKAMPFWAGEN I AUSF. A (OHNE AUFBAU)

For the tank school set up in Casarrubuelos for the duration of the war, the Germans sent a tank specially prepared for use as a driver trainer. The turret and superstructure have been removed from a line tank to enable a number of trainees to sit on an L-shaped bench.

One of the Panzer I provided by the German contingent was the one known as the 'Ohne Aufbau', or 'without superstructure', very useful for training tank drivers. (GB)

A formation of the 'Negrillo' Tank Battalion. In the foreground, the Panzer I command tank. (JMMD)

An Italian built 20mm Breda model 35 cannon. This was the weapon chosen to be fitted to the *Panzer I* to give it greater firepower against its Russian adversaries. (*JMMG*)

In any case, neither *Oberstleutnant* von Thoma nor his men liked the conversion; they went as far as calling the modified machines 'death tanks' because, in their opinion, the opening made in the turret of the converted machines to enable the gunner to aim left him dangerously exposed to enemy fire. *Oberstleutnant* von Thoma asked *Hauptmann* Wilhelmi, the aforementioned German officer liaising with Franco's headquarters, to stop the conversion of the other six tanks that *General* García Pallasar, *Comandante General de Artillería* of the CGG, had ordered to be delivered to *Teniente Coronel* Pujales late in 1937. This stop order was heeded and no more tanks were modified, much to the chagrin of *General* García Pallasar, who on 15 January 1938, sent a telegram to the 3rd Section of Franco's Staff in which he said:

The only way to remedy the defect that has been pointed out is to cover the small slot made in the armour to enable [the gunner] to aim with bullet-proof glass … In our opinion, in the light of

PANZERKAMPFWAGEN I AUSF. A 'BREDA'

Due to the German tanks' lack of firepower compared to the enemy's Russian T-26 tanks, a tank was designed to be fitted with a turret-mounted Italian 20mm 'Breda' cannon, of which finally only four vehicles were built. In the illustration we see a member of the German *Panzergruppe* in front of one of these tanks, talking to a Spanish captain wearing the uniform of the Spanish Legion.

These photographs have been much published, but they are worth including here since they clearly show the conversion carried out on the German *Panzer I* to fit the 20mm Breda cannon. Although the plan was to convert ten tanks, only four were eventually modified. Neither von Thoma nor his men liked this cannon-equipped version at all. (*GB*)

The 37mm *Panzerabwehrkanone* (PaK) 35/36 was the German army's standard anti-tank weapon in 1936. In the photo, a number of Spanish and Moroccan soldiers relax next to two of these guns. (*JMCB*)

this problem, Your Excellency [Franco] should ask himself which is more desirable: to deprive ourselves of the ability to fight enemy tanks using others capable of piercing their armour, or that von Thoma's men should run the risk of being killed in their tanks because a bullet might pass through a small gap, which anyway can and should be kept closed until it is time to aim.

Panzergruppe Drohne also added a company of anti-tank guns to each tank company so that the guns could support them against better-armed enemy tanks. Each company consisted of eight anti-tank guns, 3.7cm *Panzerabwehrkanone* (*PaK*) 35/36, each provided with its own three-axle, cross-country tractor truck, the Krupp L 2 H 43 *Protze*. There were also another five guns used as independent units, but these had to be transported on trucks.

In addition to these companies attached to tank companies, Germany sent to Spain 300 guns of the same model and calibre in a number of different consignments. These were used to form a powerful anti-tank gun group which operated on various battlefronts throughout the Civil War under the orders of *Comandante* José del Toro. As well as German materiel, the group also had Russian 45/44mm and other types of guns, all captured from the enemy.

According to a very interesting document from the *II Negociado de la 1ª Sección de la Jefatura de Movilización, Instrucción y Recuperación*, a department of the MIR, dated 12 May 1939, in addition to thirty-four Renault FT-17 tanks and seventy 'Cannon Tanks' (captured Russian T-26 Bs), there were at that time eighty-four German tanks (*Panzerkampfwagen I*) still in service and operational. From this latter figure, the one which is most relevant to this book, we can draw an important statistical conclusion. If, as we have seen, a total of 122 German tanks were delivered to Spain during the civil war, this means that only thirty-eight *Panzer I* tanks, or 31 per cent of all the tanks sent, were total losses. If we consider the twenty-nine months that these tanks were operating on battlefronts (from 1 November 1936 to the end

One of the Renault FT-17s captured during the Santander campaign. The Republican Army of the North had around thirty of these tanks, acquired by the government in Poland and mostly armed with 37mm Puteaux cannon. (*GB*)

Captures of Russian T-26B tanks by the nationalists obviated the need to provide German tanks with more firepower. The *Maestranza de Artillería* (Artillery Arsenal) in Sevilla repaired enough of these tanks to supply the armoured units on the northern and southern fronts. These units made extensive use of these tanks; nearly a hundred were distributed among companies known as '*carros-cañón*' or '*carros rusos*' (cannon tanks or Russian tanks). (*JMCB and GB*)

T-26 B TANK

The capture of a large number of these powerful Russian-built tanks by the rebel forces led to their being used in various Nationalist army tank units. The sketch shows *Comandante* José Pujales, head of the Spanish Tank Battalion, conferring with one of his captains while a Spanish artificer works behind them.

of March 1939), average total losses for *Panzer I* tanks amounted to 1.31 tanks a month, a more than acceptable figure.

If we take into account the poor performance of the German tanks combined with the overwhelming superiority of the Republicans in this type of materiel (BT-5, T-26B, BA-6, Chevrolet M.1937), we reach the inevitable conclusion that either the Nationalist tank units, aided by the German *Panzergruppe Drohne* trainers performed exceptionally well during the campaign, or their enemy, the Republican armoured and anti-tank units, did not really put up much of a fight.

The performance of the German-equipped Nationalist tank units in the first months of the conflict was less than impressive, since in terms of mobility, armour and firepower (the three key features of a successful tank) the machinery was not just unimpressive but seriously poor. But clearly machinery is not everything. Having disciplined, motivated and well-trained units infused with the morale that victory brings, able to optimally use the available resources (which included captured enemy tanks), was perhaps the key to the Nationalists' success in this area during the Spanish Civil War.

However, the Republican armoured forces were certainly no pushover, on paper at least, since they boasted over 360 tanks plus nearly 300 wheeled armoured vehicles. There can be no doubt that the Republicans did not use their armour as well as they might have done, but it cannot be denied that it was a significant enemy force.

Although the Germans were much less generous than the Russians when it came to sending armoured vehicles to Spain, the Germans were far more successful in teaching the Spanish troops how to use what they did send. Also, the Germans were much less hands-on than the Russians on the battlefield; they nearly always played an advisory role and risked the lives of their own men as little as possible (*Panzergruppe* casualties during the war were in fact remarkably low).

The German legacy could clearly be seen in Spanish post-war tank units. As well as the black beret, which is still worn today, the doctrine and the equipment would live on in the Spanish army until well into the fifties. It was not until agreements were signed with the Americans and armoured vehicles began to arrive from the other side of the Atlantic that the last of the clapped out *Panzerkampfwagen I* left over from the Civil War, by then on their last legs, were finally replaced.

The legacy left by the German *Panzergruppe*, organized by the outstanding leader Wilhelm Ritter von Thoma, was deep and enduring, and while it may be that now practically nobody in today's Spanish army will remember the origin of their modern and nimble tank units, it lies in those German merchant ships, *Girgenti* and *Passages*, which docked at the port of Sevilla on 7 October 1936.

Of all the tanks operating in the Spanish Civil War the Russian T-26B was perhaps the most commonly used. Despite its sturdiness and its powerful armament – compared to the opposition – many were captured and incorporated into Nationalist units. (*GB*)

Chapter 4

Special Training by Panzergruppe Drohne

The *Panzergruppe* instructors not only taught the Spanish how to handle tanks (driving, technique, tactics, etc.), but they also made every effort to inculcate in the Spanish troops other fundamental disciplines that were equally important in a modern, multidisciplinary war.

The special training delivered by the Germans covered such different aspects as the handling and use of flamethrowers and anti-tank guns, including Italian 47mm anti-tank guns, driving lessons for drivers of special vehicles, such as the heavy trucks of the transport company, the light *Protze* tractor trucks for pulling anti-tank guns, and courses

Throughout the campaign the *Panzergruppe Drohne* had one company of PaK 35/36 anti-tank guns. Some of the company's guns were towed by the sensational Krupp *Protze* L 2 H 43 Kfz. 69, a rear view of which can be seen in the photo. (*JMCB*)

organized for master armourers, engine mechanics and other specialists. In the following chapters we will take a closer look at the most important training groups.

The 37mm Anti-Tank Training Group

When the first two companies of *Panzerkampfwagen I Ausf. A* tanks arrived in Spain they were accompanied by twenty-four 3.7cm PaK 35/36 anti-tank guns and a group of trainers under the command of *Hauptmann* Peter Jansa.

The 3.7cm anti-tank gun was developed by the company Rheinmetall-Borsig in 1933. It was an immediate success, being adopted by the armies of a number of countries, including Italy, Holland, Japan, the USA and the Soviet Union. Although by the outbreak of the Second World War

A badge worn by the members of anti-tank gun units. (JMMG)

this gun had become obsolescent and proved largely ineffective against modern tanks, in Spain the 3.7cm PaK 35/36 was perfectly adequate against the kind of tanks that it was intended to knock out.

The backbone of the Nationalist's anti-tank defence was, without a doubt, the 37mm PaK, over 300 of which were sent to Spain. In the photo we see a gun belonging to the Tank Battalion's anti-tank battery at the Battle of Brunete. (*JMCB*)

Krupp *Protze* trucks towed the guns of two of the sections of the Tank Battalion's anti-tank company. The 3rd section's guns were carried on conventional trucks. (*GB*)

Thirteen of these first twenty-four guns to arrive in Sevilla were used to form what was known as the Motorized Anti-Tank Company, which was initially attached to the German armoured group, before being transferred to the Tank Battalion and subsequent units.

The company's eight 37mm guns each had a light, cross-country L 2 H 43 *Protze* to tow them. The other five anti-tank guns of the same model were kept back to deploy separately from the tank unit, in support of infantry columns or to defend river crossings, for example. For this reason, they were not provided with cross-country tractor trucks but instead were loaded onto trucks to be carried wherever they were needed. These first five *PaK* guns formed the embryo of what was to become the 37mm Anti-tank Gun Group which received over 300 guns during the course of the war in various consignments from Germany.

As in the case of the tanks, the anti-tank guns were sent by rail from Sevilla to Las Arguijuelas Castle (Cáceres). There, chef instructor *Hauptmann* Peter Jansa and his men started to work with the first Spanish trainees in mid-October. Franco ordered the Commander-in-Chief of the Army of the North to send *Alférez de Artillería* Pedro Sanz

KRUPP PROTZE KFZ. 69 and PAK 35/36

An anti-tank company equipped with 37mm PaK
35/36 gun fought as part of the tank unit formed by
the Germans in Spain. Their guns were pulled by the
ubiquitous and versatile *Protze* trucks, manufactured by
Krupp and put to a great many purposes. The second
lieutenant shown in the illustration belonged to a small
group of German instructors whose mission was to teach
Spanish troops how to use the German anti-tank guns.

*Panzertruppenabzeichen der
Legion Condor.* (Condor
Legion tank badge)

Their small size, lightness, and high muzzle velocity made these guns a versatile and effective weapon. Their calibre was sufficient to take on the armoured vehicles of the day, although they would soon become obsolete as the armour of the new tanks being developed was improved. (*LMF*)

From left to right: *Teniente* Valsmoreno, *Comandante* Pujales, *Alférez* Sanz and *Oberfeldwebel* Kambach. The photo was taken before the attack on the west bank of the Jarama River, on 2 February 1937. The bearded *Alférez* Pedro Sanz Ruano would become the first Spanish commander of the anti-tank company assigned to the Tank Battalion. (*JMCB*)

Ruano to Cáceres to head the new unit. With him were sent one warrant officer, five sergeants, eleven corporals, sixty gunners, twelve drivers, one carpenter, one mechanic, one mason, two clerks and eight privates, who together made up the first Spanish anti-tank unit formed by the Artillery Arm in the Nationalist zone.

As well as the aforementioned German commander of the unit, Peter Jansa, the anti-tank training unit was also staffed by *Leutnants* Gerhard Nethe, Karl Rieschick and Johann Vermeulen, *Stabsfeldwebels* Hans Novak, Martin Wolf, Hugo Ullrich and Johann Seifert, and interpreter Josef Wieseler.

A month later, on 16 November, a new training period was organized. New materiel, both anti-tank guns and tanks, wass about to arrive from Germany to be used to form three new anti-tank companies and a third *Panzer I* company to add to the two already supporting the columns advancing on Madrid.

A Russian 45mm anti-tank gun, a larger calibre copy of the German 37mm. Apart from other differences, the spoked wheels make it easy to identify. Recognizable in the top left of the photo is a full-track 'Komintern' tractor, also Russian made, captured at the Battle of Brunete along with the anti-tank gun. (*JMCB*)

Late in November, thirty-two new 3.7cm PaK guns and ten light Krupp *Protze* trucks arrived. These were used to form three anti-tank companies with ten guns each; two of the companies would have to transport their guns on the back of trucks while one company would use the new *Protze* tractor trucks to tow its guns.

In total seven officers were trained (including a captain), thirty NCOs, 120 gunners, and ten drivers. The course started in mid-December and lasted for a fortnight. Each company had ten guns with two left behind at Cubas in reserve.

The first of the companies formed and trained was the one led by *Capitán de Infantería* José del Toro, the future commander of the Spanish Anti-Tank Group. This company would be attached to the columns advancing on Madrid, replacing the first guns sent which, by then, were in urgent need of repair.

The successive deliveries of anti-tank weaponry kept *Hauptmann* Jansa's group very busy throughout the war, and the work continued even after Jansa returned to Germany on 18 March 1938.

The first anti-tank gun training courses were held in Cáceres, although they were later moved to Cubas de la Sagra and later still to the villages of Carranque and Cedillo del Condado.

Flamethrower Training

As from January 1937, *Hauptmann* Peter Jansa, chief anti-tank gun instructor, was also responsible for organizing training in the use of flamethrowers.

A much-used weapon during the First World War, flamethrowers were devices that could send a pressurized stream of inflammable liquid a certain distance. This liquid was held in a tank carried on a soldier's back and was ignited as it left the end of the nozzle, which was far enough away from the operator to prevent him getting burned by his own weapon.

A total of nine flamethrowers were supplied via the *Panzergruppe*, four light devices called *Flammenwerfer 16* or *Kleinflammenwerfer* and five of the heavier type, called trench flamethrowers by the Spanish and *Grossflammenwerfer* by the Germans. Both types had been used by the German army during the Great War.

One of the Spanish 'Bilbao' Mod. 1935 tanks used by the Germans to carry their *Grossflammenwerfer* flamethrower. We can see through the open hatch the position of the flamethrower fuel tank (behind the co-driver's seat), the flexible hose and the lance, which passed through the co-driver's window through a hole made for that purpose. A total of five of these armoured vehicles were fitted with flamethrowers. (*JMCB*)

As early as 17 October 1936, a telegram was sent from Franco's headquarters to *General* Varela asking him, 'with the utmost urgency to choose one officer and thirty soldiers from among the regiments of his columns … to be sent to La Arguijuela [sic] castle where they would be trained in the use of flamethrowers. The training timetable will established at the castle by Mr Thoma. Once their training is over they will re-join their units where they will use these devices.'

A light flamethrower known as a *Kleinflammenwerfer*. It saw widespread use by the Germans in the First World War. (*GB*)

Beret badges worn
by members of the
Panzergruppe Drohne.

'BILBAO' FLAMETHROWER TANK

The *Panzergruppe Drohne* fitted five of what the Spanish called trench flamethrowers (the heavy type) to Spanish-built armoured cars belonging to cavalry and the *Guardia de Asalto* (Assault Guard). These vehicles were sent to the Talavera front in late October where they took part in a number of operations. In the illustration we can also see a German soldier carrying a light flame thrower.

Two Spanish soldiers practising how to use the *Kleinflammenwerfer*. One carried the flamethrower fuel tank on his back while the other, further forward, aimed the lance. (*JMCB*)

In the end the training did not take place at Las Arguijuelas but at Oropesa (Toledo) instead, and nine days later the men of the Spanish legion returned to the Talavera front with their newly acquired flamethrowers.

Of the four light flamethrowers, which had an effective range of twenty-five to thirty metres, a discharge time of around ten seconds,

Panzer I Ausf. A no. 2. In place of this tank's right-hand machine gun a light flamethrower was fitted, the lance of which can be clearly seen in the photo. (*JMCB*)

The *Grossflammenwerfer* trench flamethrower and its devastating effect. (*JMCB and JMMG*)

A very interesting front view of the *Panzer I Ausf. A* no. 2. This tank was a test bed for two different types of flamethrower. As well as the German *Kleinflammenwerfer* they also tried fitting an Italian Mod. 35 flamethrower, which can be seen in this photo together with its characteristic cylindrical armour. (*RA*)

and a tank which held 11.8 litres of flammable liquid, two were delivered to *General* Varela on 24 October. Another was mounted on a *Panzerkampfwagen I Ausf. A* tank, which at 09.00 hours on 27 October left for Talavera with the rest of the tanks of the two companies and the anti-tank guns. The last flamethrower was left at Las Arguijuelas castle to be used for training purposes.

As for the five heavy flamethrowers, three of them were sent to the front at Talavera on 26 October, mounted on 'Bilbao' type armoured cars. The latter had been sent with such urgency that they arrived with a number of faults which the German workshop unit were quickly able to repair. The other two were kept at Las Arguijuelas as training aids.

A few days later, on 1 November, Varela was ordered to select fifteen men to be trained in the use of the three flamethrowers which remained at the base at Cáceres, 'Training preferably on site wherever Mr Thomas [sic] may be.' The two heavy flamethrowers would eventually be mounted on armoured cars; this work was done in Quismondo where the German tankers had set up their workshop.

A Vomag LR 448 truck towing an Sd. Ah. 115 tank transporter trailer loaded with two *Panzer I Ausf. A*, well camouflaged with branches and leaves. (*JMCB*)

The successive consignments of German materiel, acquired through the company HISMA Ltda, enabled a company of flamethrowers to be formed within the Spanish Legion unit. The company comprised three sections, two light and one heavy, each equipped with nine flamethrowers (making a total of eighteen light and nine heavy flamethrowers). At Cubas de la Sagra, von Thoma also had as many as twenty-five light and twenty heavy devices ready to be assigned to a future second company which actually never materialized. Flamethrowers were used sparingly during the Civil War; they tended to be used mainly by the Chemical Warfare Service to decontaminate impregnated areas, but were sometimes used in the fight against enemy tanks.

Training in Special Vehicles

The German army contingent of the *Heer* travelled to Spain with a large and varied amount of materiel, all of which was new to the Spanish troops and so required the organization of many training courses.

Tank transport using heavy trucks
The German transport company, commanded by *Hauptmann* Hans Schruefer throughout the war, was responsible for organizing and

Inside a workshop of the German Panzergruppe. In the foreground we see a *Panzer I Ausf. B* and behind, a *Panzerbefehlswagen I Ausf. B*. Interestingly on the rear of the command tank we can see a typical piece of workshop equipment; a metal frame which was fitted to the tank to act as a hoist so that engine could be removed. In the foreground stands *Leutnant* Paul Jaskula, head of the German workshop. (*JMCB*)

training a Spanish company to perform transport duties. One officer and seventy-five heavy truck drivers were trained in the basic requirements of this unit, such as the driving and maintenance of vehicles, general mechanics (engines, transmissions, etc.), the loading of armoured vehicles, organization of the unit, and other related matters.

Krupp L-H43 Protze Kfz 69 light truck drivers

As mentioned earlier, the vehicles chosen to tow the motorized companies' PaK artillery, were Krupp L 2 H 43 *Protze* Kfz 69 light trucks. A number of training courses were arranged for the men in the motorized companies, both those attached to the Tank Battalion and those with *Comandante* José del Toro's Anti-Tank Group. A total of thirty drivers were trained, the same number as there were '*Protze*' trucks in the *Panzergruppe*.

Workshop personnel

The *Drohne* workshop company, commanded by *Oberleutnant* Albert Schneider throughout the campaign, formed and trained a group of master mechanics, assistant master mechanics, and mechanics to work on engines and weapons. In total about eighty Spanish mechanics were trained and went on to serve in the Nationalist workshop unit or the mobile workshops of the Tank Battalion.

Chapter 5

Wheeled Vehicles of Panzergruppe Drohne

All the German units taking part in the Spanish Civil War had one thing in common: they were all fully motorized units. By the time the war ended the Condor Legion had been supplied with 322 vehicles of various types for the land contingent and 1,123 for the air contingent; a relatively meagre supply of vehicles and, as we shall see, a very mixed bag. The units sent to Spain came with their own transport; at the time the German army was re-equipping itself with all kinds of motorized vehicles, most of which had been originally designed for civilian use. This meant that the vehicles sent to Spain were from all the German manufacturers of the time and of all types and models imaginable. This was a real nightmare for maintenance services, a situation that would repeat itself on a larger scale in the Second World War.

The first expedition of the *Heer* comprised 267 men organized into one staff unit, two tank companies, a transport company, a workshop company, an anti-tank training unit, and an armoury unit. These were equipped with the following wheeled vehicles: eleven light automobiles, ten trucks for towing tank-transporter trailers (Büssing-NAG 650s), six workshop trucks (Büssing-NAG III GL6), forty-five cargo trucks (including fourteen Vomag Type 5 LR 448 tank transporters and a number of Opel Blitz trucks), nineteen Sd. Ah. 115 low-loader tank-transporter trailers, and eighteen motorcycles, as well as various trailers, water bowsers, field kitchens, etc., plus accessories and spares.

Two photos of BMW R12 motorcycles with sidecars. In the first photo we see an Opel Blitz type 2-to 3.5 and in the second photo, a *Panzerbefehlswagen I Ausf. B* command tank. (*JMMD and JMCB*)

A photo of two Stoewer R 160 Spezial taken during the Civil War in the *Plaza Mayor* of Valladolid, bearing the number plates of the Condor Legion ground forces. These were used by tank units as command vehicles. (*JMMD*)

A Horch 830 BL Sportcabriolet of the Condor Legion ground forces. (*JMMD*)

A column of Opel Blitz type 2-to 3.5 or type 2.5 to 3.5 trucks. (*JMMD*)

A Horch 830 R. Sitting in the passenger seat is the commander of the Condor Legion ground forces, *Oberst* Wilhelm Ritter von Thoma; standing next to him is the group's Chief of Staff, *Oberstleutnant* Eberhard von Ostman. (*JMMD*)

A Wanderer W11 10–50PS assigned to the German ground forces. (*JMMD*)

A Phänomen Granit 25H ambulance. (*JMMD*)

A Mercedes-Benz 320 WK belonging to the ground forces. Luggage boxes and three fuel jerrycans can be seen on the back of the car. In the background, to the left, we can see an Italian-built motorcycle. (*JMCB*)

Rear three-quarters view of a Mercedes-Benz 320 WK. (*JMMD*)

Krupp L 2 H 43 trucks. They arrived with the first Condor Legion contingent to act as tractors for anti-tank guns. (*JMCB*)

Krupp *Protze* L 2 H 43 Kfz. 69 trucks at the Zaragoza General Military Academy. They were handed over to the Spanish forces along with the tanks. These vehicles were not fitted with bumpers. (*JMMD*)

The system for loading *Panzer I* tanks onto the back of the Transport Company's trucks was simple. In this photo a *Panzer I Ausf. A* is on the ramp while to the left we catch a glimpse of the back of an *Ausf. B.* (*JMCB*)

A Büssing-NAG 650 with the old type of cab, loading a tank during the Santander campaign. (*CJMD*)

A Büssing–NAG 650 on the northern front. (*CJMD*)

A Vomag 5 LR 448 carrying a *Panzer I* and towing a UNL-35 armoured car on an Sd.Ah. 115 trailer. Behind there is a second trailer carrying fuel cans. Photographed in Aragon. (*CJMD*)

A German Sd.Ah. 115 tank transporter trailer carrying a captured T-26B. (*JMMD*)

Two Vomag 5 LR 448 trucks carrying
tanks on the northern front. (*BN*).

A convoy at halt. Each Vomag or Bussing-NAG track (the image shows the latter type) could carry two *Panzer I*: one on the truck bed and the other towed on an Sd.Ah. 115 trailer. (*JMCB*)

Two Mercedes-Benz 320 WK cars outside Avila's city walls. They are fitted with Plexiglass side screens to protect the occupants from the weather. (*JMCB*)

Vehicles of the ground forces		
Type	**Make**	**Model**
Motorcycle	BMW	R-12 with or without side-car
Car	Stoewer	R160 Spezial
Car	Horch	830 R & 830 BL
Car	Mercedes-Benz	320 WK
Car	Wanderer	W 11 10-50 PS
Truck	Büssing-NAG	650
Truck	Opel Blitz	2 To 3,5
Truck	Vomag	5LR 448
Tractor truck	Krupp	L 2H 43 "Protze"
Truck workshop	Büssing-NAG	III GL6
Ambulance	Phänomen Granit	25H
Trailer	Tank transporter	Sd. Ah. 115

Note: The vehicles mentioned here have been confirmed as having actually formed part of the unit, which is not to say that others not mentioned here may also have been used.

Workshop trucks based on Büssing-NAG III GL6 chassis, photographed in Alfaro, Logroño (present day La Rioja). Behind can be seen a trailer used as a store room. The roofs of the workshop area of each truck are different. (*JMMD*)

A Wanderer W11 12-60 PS photographed with its passengers in the early stages of the Civil War. (*JMCB*)

Vehicles & trailers of the ground forces	
Type	Quantity
Motorcycles with sidecar	32
Motorcycles	45
Light, medium and heavy vehicles	71
Special vehicles	16
Radiotelegraph & communications vehicles	8
All terrain light vehicles	4
Trucks of various types	96
Listening station trucks	2
Gasoline tanker trucks	2
Trailer trucks	15
Ambulances	3
Buses	3
Tank-transporter trailers	19
Trailers for radiotelegraphy	2
Water tanker trailer	1
Trailer for set of tools	1

Chapter 6

The Airforce Contingent

The air contingent of the Condor Legion, with its attached anti-aircraft and signals units, was by far the largest in terms of both men and vehicles. Its contribution to the Nationalist war effort, with its technologically advanced aircraft and highly skilled personnel, was unarguably decisive. Although as the war progressed much of the German materiel was passed on to the Spanish, the anti-aircraft artillery, signals equipment, and the latest model aircraft remained in the hands of the Germans throughout the conflict. Even once the war was over, most or all of the materiel which might be considered secret, such as the Junkers Ju 87 Stuka, was sent back to Germany, while the remainder, in varying states of repair, was handed over to Spanish units.

A Mercedes-Benz 290 Lang Cabriolet D belonging to S/88 (registration number LC 20065) photographed in Monzón next to an Italian Fiat 618 C truck. (*JMMD*)

A Horch 830 R car belonging to the Condor Legion, after an accident. This was one of the vehicles manufactured in 1934, featuring larger lateral cooling vents than later models. Between 1934 and 1937 the German army bought over 4,500 of these cars. (*JMMD*)

A Wanderer W23. A car widely used by the various units of the Condor Legion. (*JMMD*)

A great many vehicles were used by the most important components of the German air contingent; the fighter, bomber and reconnaissance units, the highly successful light and heavy anti-aircraft batteries, and the highly specialized motorized signals battalion. The smaller formations, such as the staff unit, the aircraft and depot support units, plus general equipment maintenance, medical and meteorological units, also used a not inconsiderable number of vehicles.

Vehicles belonging to the Condor Legion would normally have the unit to which they belonged painted on the top right corner of their windscreen, enabling each one to be easily identified. In the following sections we aim to show all the types of vehicles used by the various aviation units of the Condor Legion, mostly by means of photos taken by German soldiers involved in the war.

A Mercedes-Benz 290 Lang Cabriolet D belonging to the Condor Legion. These vehicles, originally intended for civil use, were specially bodied for the German army, using a design from coachbuilding company Erdmann & Rossi. (*JMMD*)

A Mercedes-Benz 500 Pullman-Cabriolet belonging to S/88, parked in Madrid. This is a 1932–36 version with the 100hp engine. (*CJMD*)

Vehicles of the airforce contingent	
Category	Quantity
Light vehicles	92
Medium vehicles	130
Heavy vehicles	7
Buses	4
Motorcycles	76
Motorcycles with sidecars	77
Trucks	557
Tractors	20
Special vehicles	73
Trailers	87
TOTAL	1,123

A Mercedes-Benz 290 Lang Cabriolet D, registration number LC 20069 (left), next to a Wanderer W11 12–60 PS in Òdena (Barcelona). (*JMMD*)

A Wanderer W23 belonging to the Condor Legion, photographed in Burgos. These cars began to be sold in 1937 and were widely used in Spain. (*JMMD*)

STAFF (S/88)

Known in German as *Führungsstab S/88*, this was the Condor Legion's high command, which included its commander-in-chief and staff and related services.

The Condor Legion Staff, under the direct control of the commander-in-chief, was a more streamlined organization than was normal, consisting of just two sections, Section I (with three subsections, called respectively *Ia* (command), *Ib* (operations), and *Ic* (information)) and Section II (also known as *Quartiermeister*), responsible for the logistics

A Horch 8 Type 750 B Tourenwagen (8-cylinder, 4,516cc engine delivering 90hp at 3,400rpm) photographed at Vitoria airfield with a number of German officers and a Junkers Ju 52 in the background. (*JMMD*)

services required to ensure the unit's smooth operation. The Condor Legion Staff mainly used cars originally intended for civilian use, plus a few trucks. Among the cars were some top of the range models used for special occasions together with some more modest vehicles for everyday use.

An Opel 6 belonging to the Condor Legion Staff. (*JMMD*)

A Mercedes-Benz 170V with civil coachwork. (*JMMD*)

Victory parade in Madrid 1939. A Mercedes–Benz 540 K drives along the Castellana Boulevard with an Italian general on board. (*COT*)

A BMW 326 Cabriolet. (*JMCB*)

A Wanderer 250, photographed near Avila in the winter of 1937. These cars were acquired by the German army in 1935. (*JVS*)

A Horch 830 BL belonging to S/88, off the road in San Vicente, Asturias. (*JVS*)

A Hanomag Rekord belonging to the Condor Legion in a wintery landscape. (*JMMD*)

A BMW 326 Limousine used by a high-ranking German officer in Spain. (*JMMD*)

A Mercedes-Benz 230 or 260 D with six-seater Tourenwagen coachwork. (*JMMD*)

BMW 326 Limousine in a less than pristine condition after being in an accident. It was assigned to S/88. (*CJMD*)

An excellent picture of a Horch 8 780B Pullmancabriolet with a 4,944cc 8-cylinder engine developing 100hp at 3,400rpm. It had four forward gears plus reverse. Its fuel consumption was 22l/100km with a top speed of 125kph. This Condor Legion vehicle was assigned to S/88 (Staff). *General* Sperrle, commander of the Condor Legion until October 1937, can be seen in the front passenger seat. (*JMMD*)

Generaloberst von Blomberg was appointed Minister of Defence by Hindenburg in 1933. In 1936 he would be promoted to *Generalfeldmarschall*, the first in the Nationalist-Socialist period. Two years later he would fall into disgrace after his marriage to a woman with a murky past. (*GB*)

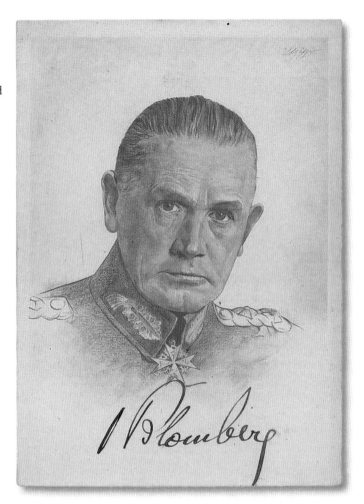

Coat of arms of the city of Neuruppin where *6.Panzer-Regiment* was based. On the right we can see the regimental insignia which decorated a plate belonging to the tableware of *6.Panzer-Regiment*. (*GB*)

The pocket battleship *Admiral Scheer*. This was one of the German warships that escorted the expedition bringing the two German armoured companies to Sevilla. (*JMCB*)

The castle of Arguijuela de Abajo.

Arguijuela de Arriba.

Medal bar with German and Spanish medals belonging to a member of the Condor Legion. (*JMCB*)

A cloth badge of one of the Navarre divisions. (*JMCB*)

Coat of arms of the *Regimiento de Infantería "Argel" no. 27*. This was a garrison regiment in Cáceres, some of whose members were used to form a tank battalion in 1936. (*GB*)

The *Cruz de Guerra* was awarded to many Germans at the end of the conflict. (*JMCB*)

A metal skull badge as worn on a tanker's black beret. (*JMCB*)

Emblem used by the armoured units of the Nationalist Army during the conflict.

Medalla Militar Individual
(*Individual Military Medal*).

A poster of the organization 'Strength through Joy' (in German '*Kraft durch Freude*'), the owner of the two merchant ships that carried the Condor Legion back to Germany. (*JMCB*)

Parade of the Condor Legion through the streets of Berlin. (*GB*)

PANZERKAMPFWAGEN I AUSF. A

On 18 October 1936, Francisco Franco, recently named *Generalísimo*, carried out an inspection of the Tank Battalion at its base at the Arguijuelas Castles (Cáceres). In the sketch we see Franco facing Wilhelm von Thoma, commander of the German contingent, and a *Panzer I* tank in the original livery of the German army.

PANZERBEFEHLSWAGEN I AUSF. B (INITIAL VERSION)

The head of the *Panzergruppe Drohne*, Wilhelm von Thoma, with the second-in-command of the 2nd Company, *Oberleutnant* Gerhard Willing, in front of one of the command tanks sent to the contingent from Germany. It is a Panzer I type 'B' in command tank configuration. These vehicles remained in Spain at the end of the war.

PANZERKAMPFWAGEN I AUSF. A (OHNE AUFBAU)

For the tank school set up in Casarrubuelos for the duration of the war, the Germans sent a tank specially prepared for use as a driver trainer. The turret and superstructure have been removed from a line tank to enable a number of trainees to sit on an L-shaped bench.

PANZERKAMPFWAGEN I AUSF. A "BREDA"

Due to the German tanks' lack of firepower compared to the enemy's Russian T-26 tanks, a tank was designed to be fitted with a turret-mounted Italian 20mm 'Breda' cannon, of which finally only four vehicles were built. In the illustration we see a member of the German *Panzergruppe* in front of one of these tanks, talking to a Spanish captain wearing the uniform of the Spanish Legion.

T-26 B TANK

The capture of a large number of these powerful Russian-built tanks by the rebel forces led to their being used in various Nationalist army tank units. The sketch shows *Comandante* José Pujales, head of the Spanish Tank Battalion, conferring with one of his captains while a Spanish artificer works behind them.

A badge worn by the members of anti-tank gun units. (JMMG)

KRUPP PROTZE KFZ. 69 and PAK 35/36

An anti-tank company equipped with 37mm PaK 35/36 gun fought as part of the tank unit formed by the Germans in Spain. Their guns were pulled by the ubiquitous and versatile Protze trucks, manufactured by Krupp and put to a great many purposes. The second lieutenant shown in the illustration belonged to a small group of German instructors whose mission was to teach Spanish troops how to use the German anti-tank guns.

Panzertruppenabzeichen der Legion Condor. (Condor Legion tank badge)

Beret badges worn
by members of the
Panzergruppe Drohne.

'BILBAO' FLAMETHROWER TANK

The *Panzergruppe Drohne* fitted five of what the Spanish called trench flamethrowers (the heavy type) to Spanish-built armoured cars belonging to cavalry and the *Guardia de Asalto* (Assault Guard). These vehicles were sent to the Talavera front in late October where they took part in a number of operations. In the illustration we can also see a German soldier carrying a light flame thrower.

Many Condor Legion units used this type of truck in various configurations. In the illustration we see the general cargo version, used by S/88, Ln/88 and F/88, and probably other units too. Also shown is a BMW R12 motorcycle.

Spanish Cross (*Spanienkreuz*) with Swords.

WANDERER W11 12-60 PS KFZ. 15
One of the most versatile medium-weight vehicles that the Germans brought to the Spanish Civil War was the Wanderer W11, with which nearly all Condor Legion units were equipped in some form or other. In this case we see one of these cars fitted out as a radio vehicle, forming part of the Ln/88 signals battalion.

MITTLERER ZUGKRAFTWAGEN (SD KFZ. 7) KM m9

These magnificent heavy tractors were used in Spain by the Condor Legion anti-aircraft group (F/88). Three different versions (KM m8, m9 and m11) were used as tractor units for the five anti-aircraft batteries equipped with 88 mm Flak 18 cannons.

The 1936-1939 campaign medal.

A Condor Legion flag.

The emblem of W/88.

Birds-eye view of a Wanderer W11 12-60 PS photographed in Sabadell. The German army received a total of 5,500 of these vehicles between 1933 and 1941. (*JMMD*)

A 1937 Wanderer W11 12-60 PS, Kfz. 12 variant, at Villafría airfield (Burgos). Behind it we can see Fieseler Storch, a Lockheed 10A Electra, and a Junkers Ju 52/3m. (*JMMD*)

A Mercedes-Benz 290 Lang Cabriolet D, belonging to the Condor Legion. The bodywork of these vehicles was specially built for the German army based on a design by coachbuilders Erdmann & Rossi. Parked behind it is a Wanderer W52, while to the right we see the rear of an Opel Olympia Cabrio-Limousine, and in the background to the right there is a Hansa-Lloyd Merkur truck. (*JMMD*)

A Hanomag Rekord Limousine on a railway flatbed. (*JMMD*)

A Wanderer W250 Limousine 6 Fenster, with coachwork by Reutter, used by S/88 of the Condor Legion.

An ambulance based on a Horch 830 BL chassis. The vast majority of German units stationed in Spain had some kind of medical vehicle. (*AGCE*)

Two-door DKW F 4 Meisterklasse, used by the Condor Legion. In the background we can see a Wanderer W23. (*JMMD*)

An Opel Blitz 3.6-42 truck. (*JMCB*)

During the Condor Legion farewell ceremony in Zaragoza, this Horch car, probably an 830 BL Tourenwagen, was used as a mobile camera platform from which to film the military parade. (*JMMD*)

A Henschel 33 G 1 used by S/88. (*JMMD*)

Vehicles of the COMMAND STAFF of the Condor Legion			
Type	Make	Model	Observations
Motorcycle	BMW	R-12	With or without sidecar
Car	Mercedes-Benz	290 lang Cabriolet D	Bodywork by Erdmann & Rossi
Car	Mercedes-Benz	500 Pullman-Cabriolet	Mod. 1932-36 motor of 100 PS
Car	Mercedes-Benz	170V	
Car	Mercedes-Benz	230-260D Tourenwagen	
Car	Mercedes-Benz	540K	
Car	Wanderer	W 23	
Car	Wanderer	W 11 12-60PS	
Car	Wanderer	W 250 Limousine 6 Fenster	Bodywork by Reutter
Car	Wanderer	W 250 Cabriolet 4 Fenster	
Car	Horch	830R	
Car	Horch	8 Type 750B Tourenwagen	
Car	Horch	830 BL Tourenwagen	
Car	Horch	8 Type 780B Pullman-Cabriolet	
Car	BMW	326 Limousine	
Car	BMW	326 Cabriolet	
Car	Hanomag	Rekord Limousine	
Car	Opel	"6"	
Car	DKW	F4 Meisterklasse Limousin	Two-door
Truck	Büssing-NAG	KD	
Truck	Opel Blitz	Type 3,6-42	
Truck	Henschel	33 G1	
Ambulance	Horch	830 BL	

Note: There is evidence that the vehicles listed here formed part of the unit, which is not say that they were the only vehicles used. They may have had other vehicles not listed here.

The Büssing-NAG KD was a variant of the standard truck (the Einheits-Diesel), 415 of which were built up to 1938. In principle this variant was intended for the export market but in the end the German army acquired all of them. The Condor Legion brought over at least ten of these trucks. (*JMMD*)

MOTORIZED AVIATION SIGNALS BATTALION (LN/88)

The German contingent included what was known as the *Luftnachrichten-Abteilung (Mot.)* or Ln/88, which made one of the most important contributions to the success of the Nationalist forces. It was equipped with a large number of special vehicles and a number of different trailers used for various tasks related to command and communications, including a great many special-bodied vehicles. This battalion was made up of four companies; one radio, one telephony, one aviation communications, and one air warning. Among other vehicles the unit used Büssing-NAG G 31, Mercedes-Benz G3a, Magirus M 206, Henschel 33, Krupp L 3 H 163 and Horch 830BL as radio trucks, as well as using similar trucks as weather stations, photographic labs, telephony switchboards, teletype and telegraph transceivers, printing presses, etc. Communications engineers used Krupp L 3 H 163 trucks and Hanomag 4/20 PS Typ 63 and Hanomag Garant cars to lay telephone cables.

Rear view of a Büssing–NAG G 31. In the photo the rear compartment, used as a storeroom, is open. In the centre of the photo a German soldier is using a pedal-driven generator. The truck on the left of the photo has its radio mast, attached to rear of vehicle, fully extended. The vehicle further away from the camera has a smaller radio mast. (*JMMD*)

A Mercedes-Benz 170 or 200 Cabriolet C belonging to 1.Ln/88. (*AGCE*)

A Vomag 5 LR 448 converted into a radio station. This vehicle had a straight front bumper. (*ME*)

A Hanomag Garant at an airfield used by the Condor Legion. (*CJMD*)

A Hanomag Garant belonging to the Condor Legion, by the Ebro River. (*JMMD*)

A Hanomag Garant belonging to 1.Ln/88, with Kfz. 2 bodywork, next to a large trailer. The photograph was taken in Alcañiz. (*JMMD*)

A Hanomag Garant Kfz. 2. (*AGCE*)

Several Hanomag Garant Kfz. 2 communications vehicles. (*AGCE*)

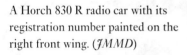

A Horch 830 R radio car with its registration number painted on the right front wing. (*JMMD*)

A Mercedes–Benz Stuttgart 260 photographed in northern Spain. Parked next to it is a BMW 309 converted for use as a telephone line laying vehicle (Kfz. 2). (*JMMD*)

A Wanderer W250 Cabriolet 4 Fenster (1936) photographed in Fitero (Navarra). It was equipped with bodywork designed by Gläser and a 6-cylinder, 50hp, 2,255cc engine. This particular vehicle was assigned to the Staff of the Motorized Signals Battalion (St.Ln/88) of the Condor Legion. A metal equipment box and a fuel jerrycan have been attached to each running board. (*JMMD*)

A Horch 8 500B heads a column of Condor Legion signals vehicles. (*JMMD*)

A large number of German are lined up prior to the Barajas parade, including several signals vehicles. (*JMMD*)

A Hanomag Garant Kfz. 2 next to a Zündapp K 800. (*JMMD*)

A Horch 830 R. (*JMCB*)

A Horch 830 R. (*JMMD*)

A Horch 830 R fitted out as a Kfz. 17 radio vehicle. The letters J/H have been painted on the windshield, but we are unaware of their significance. (*JMMD*)

A Wanderer W11 12-60 PS, Kfz. 15 variant. The photo was probably taken in Zaragoza. (*JMMD*)

Spanish Cross (*Spanienkreuz*) with Swords.

WANDERER W11 12-60 PS KFZ. 15

One of the most versatile medium-weight vehicles that the Germans brought to the Spanish Civil War was the Wanderer W11, with which nearly all Condor Legion units were equipped in some form or other. In this case we see one of these cars fitted out as a radio vehicle, forming part of the Ln/88 signals battalion.

A group of Condor Legion signals vehicles, including two Büssing-NAG G 31 signals vans and an Opel 3.6–36 truck. (*JMMD*)

A Büssing-NAG G 31 Kfz. 61. The design of the front wings are of a more modern type. (*JMMD*)

A German signals unit stationed in the Plaza de la Creu Alta, in Sabadell. Two Büssing-NAG G 31 trucks can be seen alongside two Krupp L 3 H 63. (*JMMD*)

A group of Condor Legion signals vehicles, including two Büssing-NAG G 31 signals vans and an Opel 3.6-36 truck. (*JMMD*)

A Büssing-NAG G 31 Kfz. 61. (*JMMD*)

A Mercedes-Benz G3a with the most modern bodywork they were fitted with. It belonged to the 1st Company Ln/88 (*JMMD*)

A signals unit of the Condor Legion. In this photo we can see part of the signals equipment that Germany sent to the rebel forces (*JMCB*)

A Mercedes-Benz G3a of Ln/88 with some other German vehicles. (*JMMD*)

A truck used by the Condor Legion as a radio vehicle, fitted with a tall mast. Next to it there is an Sd.Ah. 24 generator set. We are unaware of the make and model of the truck, although it may be a captured vehicle. (*JMMD*)

A Z1 truck, used by the Ln/88, photographed with a motorcycle BMW R12. (*JMMD*)

A Krupp L 3 H 163 of the 1.Ln/88. (*AGCE*)

Krupp L 3 H 63 camouflaged with netting, photographed in Quintanapalla, Burgos. (*JMMD*)

A Krupp L 3 H 63 in Kfz. 72 configuration, belonging to 2.Ln/88. On the ground we can see the small generator that radio trucks were equipped with. The winch cable guide can be seen under the right-hand headlamp. (*JMMD*)

Right hand side view of a Krupp L 3 H 63. (*JMMD*)

A Krupp L 3 H 63 used as a heavy radio vehicle Kfz. 72 by 2.Ln/88. (*JMMD*)

Rear three quarters view of a Krupp L 3 H 63 Kfz. 72, used as a radio vehicle. (*JMMD*)

A column of vehicles of the Condor Legion with a Hanomag Garant followed by a Büssing-NAG G 31 fitted out as a telephone truck (Kfz. 77). (*JMMD*)

Büssing-NAG G 31 trucks with bodywork especially designed to be used for laying telephone lines. A number of these vehicles arrived in Spain for the exclusive use of the Condor Legion. (*JMMD*)

In this interesting photo of the Signals Battalion of the Condor Legion, to the left we can see two Henschel 33 D1 trucks configured as radio vehicles (Kfz. 72). The bumpers, with a cylindrical upper bar, show them to be the Type 4 version. (*JMMD*)

A Henschel 33 D1 truck with a body designed for the laying of telephone lines, belonging to the German signals unit in Spain. (*AGCE*)

A Henschel 33 belonging to 1.Ln/88 fitted out as heavy Kfz. 72 signals trucks, parked in Alcañiz (Teruel) in August 1938. The lateral awnings that the German signals vehicles were fitted with can be seen here extended. They are probably teletype trucks (*Fernschreibkraftwagen*). (*JMMD*)

Many Condor Legion units used this type of truck in various configurations. In the illustration we see the general cargo version, used by S/88, Ln/88 and F/88, and probably other units too. Also shown is a BMW R12 motorcycle.

A Magirus M206 belonging to the Condor Legion, configured as a radio vehicle (Kfz. 61). (*JMMD*)

A Magirus M30 used by the Condor Legion as a telecommunications workshop (Kfz. 42). (*AGCE*)

A Magirus M206. This was a version not often seen, with bodywork designed for carrying a radio mast (Kfz. 68). On the roof of the cab we can see the cowling to protect the end of the mast, which lay flat on the roof of the truck when in transit. (*JMMD*)

Rear view of a Magirus M206 Kfz. 61. The radio mast can be seen attached to the rear panel. (*JMMD*)

A Magirus M206 Kfz. 61 next to a Horch 830 R Kfz. 17, both belonging to the Motorized Signals Battalion. (*JMMD*)

A convoy of Condor Legion vehicles. Second in line is a Krupp L 2 H 43 Kfz. 61.

A convoy of Condor Legion vehicles. Second in line is a Krupp L 2 H 43 Kfz. 61. (*JMMD*)

Rear view of a Krupp L 2 H 43 Kfz. 61.(*JMCB*)

A Krupp L 2 H 43 in Kfz. 61 configuration, photographed in Ávila. (*JMMD*)

A Krupp L 2 H 43 with radio van bodywork (Kfz. 61). Behind is a Büssing-NAG G 31. Both belonged to 1.Ln/88. (*JMMD*)

A Kfz. 61 radio vehicle on a Krupp L 2 H 43 chassis, heavily camouflaged with tree branches. (*JMMD*)

A Krupp L 2 H 43 in Kfz. 68 radio mast truck configuration, belonging to 4.Ln/88. At the top of the rear panel we can see where the mast was anchored, while at each bottom corner there is a stabilizing jack. The photo was taken in San Rafael del Río (Castellón), near La Sénia. (*JMMD*)

In this photograph we can
see a folded radio mast
lying in a recess in the roof
a Krupp L 2 H 43 Kfz. 68.
(*JMMD*)

A Magirus M206 belonging to 3.Ln/88
photographed in Amposta. (*JMMD*)

A Magirus M206 of the Condor Legion's
Motorized Signals Battalion. (*JMMD*)

Vehicles of the of the Condor Legion signals group		
Type	Make	Model
Motorcycle	Zundapp	K-800
Motorcycle	BMW	R 12
Car	Mercedes-Benz	170
Car	Mercedes-Benz	200 Cabriolet
Car	Mercedes-Benz	Stuttgart 260/
Car	Wanderer	W 11 12-60PS
Car	Wanderer	W 250 Cabriolet 4 Fenster
Car	Horch	830R
Car	BMW	309
Car	BMW	315 Cabriolet
Car	Hanomag	Garant (various bodyworks)
Truck	Büssing-NAG	G-31 (various versions)
Truck	Vomag	5LR-448 (converted)
Truck	Henschel	33 D (various versions)
Truck	Henschel	33 G (various versions)
Truck	Mercedes-Benz	G3a
Truck	Magirus	M 206
Truck	Magirus	M 30
Truck	MAN	Z1
Truck	Krupp	L2 H 43
Truck	Krupp	L3 H 63
Truck	Krupp	L3 H 163
Trailer	—	Sd. Ah. 447
Trailer	—	Sd. Ah. 422

A van of an unidentified make, fitted out as a mobile radio station for use by the Condor Legion. (*JMMD*)

Note: There is evidence that the vehicles listed here formed part of the unit, which is not say that they were the only vehicles used. They may have had other vehicles not listed here.

A Mercedes-Benz Stuttgart 260 belonging to an anti-aircraft unit stationed in Vitoria. Behind is a 1931 Hanomag 4/20 PS Type 63 with Cabriolet-Limousine coachwork, and a 12-tonne Sd.Kfz. 7 half-track. (*JMMD*)

MOTORIZED ANTI-AIRCRAFT BATTALION (F/88)

The *Flak-Abteilung (mot.) F/88* (Motorized anti-aircraft artillery battalion) initially consisted of one 20mm light battery and one 88mm heavy battery, but by the end of 1936 it boasted two 20mm and four 88mm batteries (one more in 1938) as well as a munitions battery, a searchlight and sound locator battery, and a training battery for instructing Spanish recruits.

Among the first weapons received by the Franquist forces in August 1936 were a number of 88mm anti-aircraft guns. These guns, which were later to gain fame during the Second World War, played a decisive role in the Spanish war. Their great versatility made them effective against land targets, whether heavily fortified positions or armoured vehicles. These artillery pieces were organized into batteries of four guns each; the actual number of batteries varied as the war progressed. F/88's batteries, equipped with 88mm guns, were towed by their own special vehicle, the Sdkfz 7 half-track. Just twenty of these tractors of varying types arrived in Spain, which meant that Henschel 6x4 trucks had to be pressed into service to tow some of the guns. These trucks were also used to tow 37mm guns and a significant number of Krupp L 2 H 143 were employed to pull the light 20mm guns.

In addition to these vehicles the anti-aircraft batteries used motorcycles with or without sidecars, non-military vehicles, some of which were customized for military use, and various communications vehicles similar to those used by Ln/88.

Mercedes-Benz N46 trucks belonging to 7.F/88 (Munitions Column) which arrived late in 1936. They were fitted with bodywork used by the German police as police vans (*Polizei-Mannschaftswagen*) but in Spain they were used as cargo trucks for the German anti-aircraft batteries. (*HH*)

An image taken in the River Pisuerga, in the town of Alar del Rey (Palencia), in 1937, in which we see a Büssing–NAG G 31 chassis fitted with a cargo body next to a Mercedes-Benz Lo 3500 bus. (*JMMD*)

A Mercedes-Benz Stuttgart 260 used as a medical vehicle by a German anti-aircraft battery during the Battle of the Ebro. Their headlamps were fitted with covers for travelling at night under blackout conditions. (*JMMD*)

An interesting photograph showing a little seen vehicle; a Mercedes-Benz O 3000 (L57) from 1930-31, fitted with 25-seater *Polizei-Mannschaftswagen* bodywork. It was powered by a 6-cylinder 4,160cc M 56 engine delivering 70hp. The motorcycle is a BMW R12. (*JMMD*)

A BMW R12 with sidecar next to a Mittlerer Zugkraftwagen 8t Sd Kfz. 7 KM m 8. On the left is a Mercedes-Benz Stuttgart 260. (*JMMD*)

A Horch 8 Type 500B assigned to the German anti-aircraft group. (*JMMD*)

A Victoria KR 6 Bergmeister motorcycle belonging to 2.F/88. (*JMMD*)

A Horch 830 R with Kfz. 17 bodywork belonging to 2.F/88, photographed in Vinaròs. (*JMMD*)

A number of BMW 309 (Kfz. 2) cars used by 6.F/88. This unit was the searchlight battery of the Condor Legion's anti-aircraft group. It was equipped with 150cm searchlights and Elascop RRH listening devices. (*JMMD*)

A BMW 309 (Kfz. 2), manufactured in 1935. The bodywork was designed by Magirus. (*JMMD*)

A BMW 309 fitted with a body for laying telephone lines (Kfz. 2). Between 1929 and 1936 the German army acquired around 2,000 BMW cars. (JMMD)

This photograph taken in Vitoria gives us an excellent view of a Hansa–Lloyd Merkur III truck parked between a truck and a half-track belonging to F/88. Immediately behind it is a Mercedes-Benz 170 or 200. The type 170 (fitted with a 1,692cc, 6-cylinder Daimler-Benz M15 engine delivering 32hp) was externally identical to the type 200. (*JMMD*)

A BMW 3/20 PS Tourenwagen belonging to 1.F/88. The bodywork was designed by the coachbuilders Sindelfingen. It has been adapted for military use with the addition of a fuel jerrycan on the running board. (*JMCB*)

A Wanderer W11 12–60 PS photographed in Bilbao. (*JMMD*)

Several Hanomag Garants used by 6.F/88. (*JMMD*)

A Phänomen Granit 25H ambulance attached to 2.F/88. (*JMMD*)

Photo of an Opel Blitz 2-to 3.5 ambulance belonging to F/88, photographed in Asturias.
(*JMCB*)

A Horch 830 BL ambulance.
(*JMMD*)

A Horch 830 BL with a Kfz. 31 body. (*JMMD*)

A Wanderer W11 12-60 PS. This is the Kfz. 15 bodied version, as can be seen from the communications equipment and the radio mast on the back of the vehicle. It was assigned to 8.F/88. Right behind it is a Horch 901. (*JMMD*)

Front view of a
Krupp L 2 H 43.
Lettering on the
windscreen identifies
it as belonging to
5.F/88. (*JMMD*)

A Krupp L 3 H 143 belonging
to a German anti-aircraft
battery. (*JMMD*)

A 20mm Flak 30 anti-aircraft battery being towed by Krupp L 2 H 143 trucks.

A Krupp L 2 H 143 belonging to 4.F/88. Each German light anti-aircraft battery had sixteen 20 mm Flak 30 guns. (*JMMD*)

A light anti-aircraft battery of the Condor Legion, towed by Krupp L 2 H 143 trucks, crossing a river, probably during the Cataluña offensive. (*JMMD*)

Two Krupp L 2 H 143 trucks hit by an Italian bombing raid at Munguía in June 1937. A number of soldiers were killed in this action and 5.F/88 lost several vehicles. (*JMMD*)

A couple of Krupp L 2 H 143 belonging to 5.F/88 photographed in Ribadesella, Asturias. The picture clearly shows the camouflaged canvas covers on the back of the trucks. (*JMMD*)

Henschel 33 trucks were used as artillery tractors by the Condor Legion and by the Nationalists, which acquired a large number of these vehicles. (*JMMD*)

On the right of this interesting photograph of 8.F/88 we can see a rear view of a Kfz. 74 truck, probably a Krupp L 3 H 163, used for carrying equipment for 88 mm anti-aircraft guns, towing a trailer. In the middle of the trailer box we can see the protective housing for a 4-metre rangefinder; to the left we see a listening device. (*JMMD*)

A Krupp L 3 H 163 fitted out as a anti-aircraft artillery support vehicle (Kfz. 74), photographed in La Sénia. (*JMMD*)

León railway station. In the foreground there are a number of Krupp L 2 H 143 trucks loaded onto flatbed, with a three-colour camouflage scheme. (*JMMD*)

A Henschel 33 D1 towing an 88mm gun. These trucks were often used for this purpose due to the lack of half-tracks, although their off-road capabilities were limited. Franco's army acquired a large consignment of these vehicles from Germany to pull German 88 mm and 75 mm anti-aircraft guns. (*JMMD*)

A light 37mm Flak 18 cannon with its tractor: a Henschel 33 truck. (*JMMD*)

Front view of a Henschel 33 B 1. The radiator was narrower than the ones fitted to D and G type trucks. It was fitted with a type B, 4-cylinder, 7,188cc petrol engine delivering 60hp. The bonnet over the engine was shorter than in the D or G type trucks and the left-hand side cooling vents were different because there was a bulge at the bottom. It was not fitted with the original three-spoke wheels but had the same wheels as the D and G types. It had a shorter wheelbase (3,400mm) and the windscreen was fixed; it could not be folded down onto the bonnet. (*JMMD*)

MITTLERER ZUGKRAFTWAGEN (SD KFZ. 7) KM m9

These magnificent heavy tractors were used in Spain by the Condor Legion anti-aircraft group (F/88). Three different versions (KM m8, m9 and m11) were used as tractor units for the five anti-aircraft batteries equipped with 88 mm Flak 18 cannons.

The 1936–1939 campaign medal.

A Condor Legion flag.

Two Mittlerer Zugkraftwagen 8-to (Sd. Kfz. 7) Typ KM m8 tractors belonging to 2.F/88. They are fitted with canvas and Plexiglas screens to protect the crew from bad weather. (*JMMD*)

In this photo taken in Aragón we can see a Mittlerer Zugkraftwagen 8-to (Sd. Kfz. 7) Typ KM m8 belonging to 2.F/ 88. In this vehicle the rear track guard bulged outwards, meaning this was the 1935 version. (*JMMD*)

This photograph shows some of the vehicles used by the 8th Battery of the Condor Legion anti-aircraft group. Nearest the camera is a Wanderer W23, next is a Mercedes-Benz 170 V, then come three Wanderer W11 12-60 PS and four Mittlerer Zugkraftwagen 8-to (Sd. Kfz. 7) KM m8 tractors. (*JMMD*)

Vehicles belonging to 3.F/88 in Vitoria. On the right is a Mittlerer Zugkraftwagen 8-to (Sd. Kfz. 7). On the left a Krupp L 3 H 163 Kfz. 74. (*JMMD*)

A Krauss-Maffei (Sd. Kfz. 7) KM m8 belonging to 8.F/88 in trouble in the middle of a river after slipping down the riverbank. Some vehicles were fitted with outsize air filters fitted on either side of the bonnet. (*JMMD*)

Rear view of an Sd. Kfz. 7 KM m8 half-track. (*JMMD*)

A Krupp L 3H 163 with a tank mounted on the truck bed, for supplying the 8.F/88's Krauss-Maffei tractors with fuel. (*JMMD*)

A Mittlerer Zugkraftwagen 8-to (Sd. Kfz. 7) Typ KM m9 sporting one of the various paint schemes used during the conflict. (*JMMD*)

Another half-track of the same type, belonging to 1.F/88. (*JMMD*)

In this case the KM m9 tractor was assigned to 2.F/88. The image was taken in the outskirts of Alfaro, La Rioja. (*JMMD*)

A Krauss–Maffei KM m9 half-track belonging to 2.F/ 88, stuck in the mud. (*JMMD*)

A Mittlerer Zugkraftwagen 8-to (Sd. Kfz. 7) KM m9. The front of this version was completely different from that of the previous KM m8 version. (*JMMD*)

A Sd. Kfz. 7 KM m 9, belonging to the 3rd Battery F/88, crosses a provisional bridge towing an 88 mm Flak 18 anti-aircraft gun. (*JMMD*)

An anti-aircraft battery equipped with 88 mm cannons, probably 3.F/88. This photo shows a number of different vehicles among which are four tractors, three of them KM m9 and on KM m11. In the foreground are two 3-axle Henschel trucks each towing a 20mm Flak 30 gun belonging to the battery, whose job it was to defend the battery against low-level enemy attacks. (*JMMD*)

A Krauss–Maffei (Sd. Kfz. 7) KM m11 tractor photographed in 1938 next to an older model (KM m8) on the right, both belonging to 2.F/88. At least four of these tractors were distributed among the various batteries to replace vehicles lost during the war. (*JMMD*)

A listening device deployed at Vitoria airfield. (*JMMD*)

RRH listening devices and Type 36 fire control directors were mounted on Sd.Ah.104 trailers. The photo shows one of the latter devices, covered by a tarpaulin, in Calanda, Teruel. (*JMMD*)

In the foreground we see a Type 36 fire control director used by 88/56 Flak 18 anti-aircraft guns. Immediately behind are two half-tracks; a Krauss–Maffei (Sd. Kfz. 7) KM m11 (left) and KM m9 (right), ready to take part in a parade. The photo was probably taken in Barcelona. (*JMMD*)

A listening device photographed in the north of Spain being towed by a Krupp L 3 H 163 truck. (*JMMD*)

An Sd.Ah.104 trailer and a Type 36 fire control director with a 4-metre rangefinder in place. The rangefinder would be carried disassembled on a Kfz. 74 truck. (*JMMD*)

Vehicles of the Condor Legion anti-aircraft group		
Type	**Make**	**Model**
Motorcycle	**Victoria**	**KR6 Bergmeister**
Motorcycle	BMW	R 12
Car	Mercedes-Benz	170 V
Car	Mercedes-Benz	Stuttgart 260
Car	Wanderer	W 11 12-60PS
Car	Wanderer	W 23
Car	Horch	830R
Car	Horch	8 Type 500B
Car	Horch	901
Car	BMW	309
Car	BMW	3/20 PS Tourenwagen
Car	Hanomag	4/20 Limousine
Car	Hanomag	Garant (various bodyworks)
Truck	Büssing-NAG	G-31 (various versions)
Truck	Hansa-Lloyd	Merkur III
Truck	Henschel	33 D1
Truck	Henschel	33G1
Truck	Henschel	33 B1
Truck	Mercedes-Benz	N 46
Truck	Mercedes-Benz	O 3000 (L 57)
Truck	Krupp	L2 H 43
Truck	Krupp	L3 H 163
Bus	Mercedes	Lo 3500
Ambulance	Phänomen-Granit	25H
Ambulance	Opel- Blitz	2To 3,5
Ambulance	Horch	830 BL
Heavy tractor	Krauss-Maffei	KM m8, m9 & m11

An Opel 20-12 photographed at Burgos airfield next to a damaged '*Bacalao*'. (*JMMD*)

OPERATIONAL SQUADRON VEHICLES

This chapter examines some of the various types of vehicles used by the German operational flying units during the Spanish Civil War.

These units include *Kampfgruppe K.88*, a bomber group that had three staffeln, squadrons, of twelve aircraft apiece. For a short time, an experimental bomber unit, *Versuchsbomberstaffel 88*, was allocated to *K.88*, giving rise, in time, to a fourth squadron. A small force of Junkers Ju 87 dive-bombers also formed part of *K.88*, this being referred to as *Stuka 88*.

The fighter coverage was provided by *Jagdgruppe 88*, more commonly referred to as *J./88*. Comprising of three to four staffeln, each with a strength of twelve aircraft, *J./88* was also allocated a fighter test squadron, this being named *Versuchsjagdstaffel 88*.

The air reconnaissance role was performed by the crews of *Aufklärungsgruppe 88* (*A./88*). This generally comprised twelve aircraft, though this did vary throughout the duration of the fighting.

The final main aerial element was provided by *Gemischte Aufklärungs und Bombenstaffel (See) 88*, or *AS//88*. This squadron, which had a minimum of six seaplanes of various types, was employed on maritime reconnaissance and bombing duties.

A Magirus M37 truck used to move the cumbersome fuselage of a Junkers Ju 86 D-1 of the VB/88 Experimental Bomber Group. (*JMCB*)

A Magirus M37 truck of the unit supporting one of the Condor Legion bomber squadrons. (*JMMD*)

A Mercedes-Benz LG 3000 Kfz. 384 tanker truck after an accident. The exhaust pipe can be seen, routed under the running board. Road accidents were frequent, resulting in a large number of write-offs. The Phänomen Granit 25H ambulance on the road behind is fitted with a central headlamp instead of the normal headlamps fitted just inside the front wings. (*JMMD*)

A Mercedes-Benz LG 3000 Kfz. 384 without the front-mounted winch. Painted on the side is the date of the fall of Madrid and the words 'Free Madrid' in German. (*JMMD*)

A Mercedes-Benz LG 3000 Kfz. 384 photographed in La Sénia. (*JMMD*)

A Mercedes-Benz LG 3000 Kfz. 384. (*JMMD*)

A Mercedes-Benz Lo 2750 of the 3.K/88. (*JMMD*)

A Rear view of a Krupp L 3 H 163 Kfz. 354. (*JMMD*)

A tanker trailer used by the Condor Legion, photographed refuelling a Junkers Ju 52/3m ge bomber. It is a commercially designed trailer (*Schwerer Anhänger mit Betriebsstoff-Kesselanlage*). (*JMMD*)

A Mercedes-Benz Lo 3000 belonging to a German bomber unit, photographed in Zaragoza. (*JMMD*)

A BMW R 4 with sidecar belonging to a German bomber squadron. (*JMMD*)

A Mercedes-Benz G3a truck photographed in Oviedo with airfield guidance equipment. (*JMMD*)

An Opel Blitz 2-to 3.5 truck with a military cab, fitted out to run on producer gas. In the photo the generator had been dismantled. (*HGE*)

A member of the Condor Legion cleaning a FAUN L 354 truck, using what looks like a forerunner of the modern mop. (*JMMD*)

A Vomag 5 LR 448 truck. This vehicle was classified as a heavy truck and was used for various tasks, such as the transport of large aircraft parts. The truck in this photo, taken in 1938, is carrying the wing of a Junkers Ju 52 3m belonging to Iberia and has its cab bodywork removed. (*JMMD*)

German D1 buses. The first one has the emblem of 1.K/88 painted on the side. (*JMMD*)

A Vomag 4 OR off the road in the north of Spain. It was assigned to 2.K/88. (*JMMD*)

A Mercedes-Benz Lo 2750 bus of the Condor Legion photographed in Burgos after a heavy snowfall. (*JMMD*)

A wrecked D1 bus belonging to 3.K/88. (*JMMD*)

A column of German vehicles led by a Mercedes-Benz L 5000 truck followed by a Magirus M37. (*ME*)

An engine pre-heater (*Einbrennergerät; B-Reihe mit Zweiachsfahrgestell*). The letter F in this case was used to identify the various vehicles forming part of the airfield operations units assigned to each German squadron. (*JMMD*)

A Büssing–NAG G 31 with a cargo truck body. (*JMCB*)

A Mercedes–Benz Stuttgart 260 used by the A/88. (*JMMD*)

A Hansa-Lloyd Merkur III. (*JMMD*)

An Opel 2.0 litre '6', belonging to 2.J/88, with the unit's top hat symbol on the right front wing and an unusual registration number. (*JMMD*)

An Opel Blitz 3.6–36 S. The right front wing bears the emblem of 4.J/88. It was fitted with the second type of cargo bed used by these trucks, designed for the transport of goods. (*JMMD*)

A Vomag 5 LR 448 belonging to the Condor Legion, carrying a Messerschmitt Bf 109 B-2 flown by 2.J/88. (*JMMD*)

A Vomag 5 LR 448 next to a crash-landed Heinkel He 51 B. (*JMMD*)

This photograph was taken in Sabadell, Barcelona, in 1939. It shows a Büssing-NAG truck, probably a 350 type (fitted with a Maybach OS 7, 6-cylinder, 6,995cc, petrol engine developing 80hp at 1,200rpm), carrying a field kitchen. This truck was one of the vehicles made in 1933/34 with a cab fitted with high, narrow side-windows. (*JMMD*)

Vehicles of the Condor Legion's squadrons		
Type	**Make**	**Model**
Motorcycle	BMW	R 4
Car	Mercedes-Benz	Stuttgart 260/
Car	Opel	2.0 litre "6"
Truck	Büssing-NAG	G-31
Truck	Hansa-Lloyd	Merkur III
Truck	Vomag	3LR 443
Truck	Vomag	5LR 448
Truck	Mercedes-Benz	G3a
Truck	Mercedes-Benz	Lo 2750)
Truck	Mercedes-Benz	Lo 3000
Truck	Krupp	L3 H 163
Truck	Magirus	M 37
Truck	Faun	L 354
Truck	Opel	Blitz 3,6-36S
Truck	Opel	Blitz 2 To 3,5
Truck	Opel	2,0 12
Tanker truck	Mercedes-Benz	LG 3000
Bus	MAN	D1
Ambulance	Phänomen-Granit	25H

Note: There is evidence that the vehicles listed here formed part of the unit, which is not say that they were the only vehicles used. They may have had other vehicles not listed here.

Vehicles of the Condor Legion depot		
Type	**Make**	**Model**
Motorcycle	Zundapp	K 800
Truck	Büssing-NAG	300
Truck	Büssing-NAG	502
Truck	Vomag	3LR 443
Truck	Mercedes-Benz	G3a
Truck	Mercedes-Benz	Lo 2750)
Truck	Krupp	L3 H 63
Truck	MAN	Z1
Truck	Opel	Blitz 3,6-42
Truck	Opel	Blitz 3,6-36
Truck	Opel	2,0-12
Truck	Ford	817T
Mobile crane	Krupp	L3 H 63
Truck workshop	Daimler	DR 4-5
Tractor	FAMO	Rübezahl
Tractor	Hanomag	RD 36

Note: There is evidence that the vehicles listed here formed part of the unit, which is not say that they were the only vehicles used. They may have had other vehicles not listed here.

A Zündapp K 800 motorcycle with sidecar assigned to P/88. (*JMMD*)

MAINTENANCE GROUP (P./88)

The Air Maintenance Group and Depot (*Luftzeuggruppe und Luftpark, P./88*) was a Condor Legion support unit responsible for aircraft maintenance and repair, and the rescue and recovery of damaged aircraft.

This unit was formed of three companies, called 1.P/88, 2.P/88 and 3.P/88. It was equipped with a large number of vehicles whose purpose was to recover vehicles and aircraft used by the air contingent. It also had a great many general-purpose trucks as the unit also served as a transport reserve unit.

A column of Mercedes-Benz trucks, probably an Lo 2750s, photographed in Segovia. (*JMMD*)

A Mercedes-Benz, probably an Lo 2750, belonging to the Condor Legion. (*JMMD*)

Front view of a
Vomag 3 LR 443
truck. (*JMMD*)

A column of Opel Blitz 3.6-36 S. (*JMMD*)

An Opel Blitz 3.6–36 S. This one is fitted with the first type of this truck bed, designed for carrying troops, with fixed benches running along either side and cargo boxes bolted to the truck bed for storing the soldiers' equipment. This layout made the truck unsuitable for transporting cargo. (*JMMD*)

Several Opel Blitz belonging to the Condor Legion; in the foreground a 3.6–42 with two 3.6–36 types behind. (*JMMD*)

A Büssing-NAG, probably a 300, parked in Sabadell (Barcelona). (*JMMD*)

A MAN Z1. (*JMMD*)

Fifteen or so Opel Blitz 3.6-42 at a depot in Zaragoza. (*JMMD*)

An Opel 2,0–12 belonging to P/88. (*JMMD*)

Franco's troops were not the only ones to use Ford 817T trucks. The photo shows a Condor Legion column containing a number of these trucks. (*JMMD*)

A Mercedes-Benz G3a truck photographed during an operation to recover a crashed aircraft. (*JMMD*)

A Mercedes-Benz G3a photographed in the north of Spain. (*JMMD*)

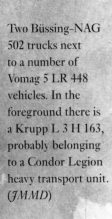

Two Büssing-NAG 502 trucks next to a number of Vomag 5 LR 448 vehicles. In the foreground there is a Krupp L 3 H 163, probably belonging to a Condor Legion heavy transport unit. (*JMMD*)

Among the different versions of Krupp L 3 H 63 trucks that the Condor Legion used in Spain was a mobile crane designed to change aircraft engines. In this picture we see three units parked in a town near to León, with the crane covered by a large tarpaulin. (*JMMD*)

An interesting photograph taken in Spain, probably at the end of the war. It shows a Kfz. 51 workshop truck based on a Daimler DR 4-5 (powered by a 4-cylinder, 7,230cc Daimler La 1264 K engine developing 50hp at 1,000rpm, with a maximum speed 18kph and a payload of 4,000/5,000kg), loaded on an MZA railway flatbed. These vehicles were acquired by the *Reichswehr* during the twenties. (*JMMD*)

A crane used by the Condor Legion at León airfield. It was used to assemble aircraft that would arrive packed in large wooden crates. (*JMMD*)

A Kfz. 75 crane belonging to the Condor Legion, mounted on a Krupp L 3 H 163. On its right we see one of the Mercedes-Benz L 3750 trucks bought by the Nationalist army in 1937. (*JMMD*)

A workshop trailer used by the Condor Legion. On the left, Heinkel He 51 fighter planes. (*JMMD*)

A Henschel 33 D1 Kfz. 75 mobile crane photographed near Lleida. (*Collection of José Manuel Campesino Bilbao*)

A FAMO Rübezahl crawler tractor belonging to P/88 next to a crash-landed Heinkel He 111. (*JMMD*)

A rear view of a Büssing-NAG 502 fitted out as a mobile workshop and two small trailers used as parts stores. (*JMMD*)

A FAMO Rübezahl crawler tractor. (*JMMD*)

A FAMO Rübezahl crawler tractor at León airfield. (*JMMD*)

In the background can be seen a Büssing-NAG ES. (*JMMD*)

A Hanomag RD 36 tractor photographed in Vitoria. Behind there is a Henschel-engine workshop truck and a number of large workshop trailers. (*JMMD*)

A Hanomag RD 36 tractor towing a tanker trailer, photographed next to a Heinkel He 111, probably at Zaragoza airfield. On the tractor's radiator grill there is a Mercedes-Benz badge, suggesting that its original engine had been replaced by a Mercedes unit. (*JMMD*)

In Spain the Germans used large trailers, similar to the ones used by the circuses of the day, with solid-tyred wheels. These trailers served as offices, stores, and workshops supporting Condor Legion squadrons. (*JMMD*)

Rear view of one of the workshop trailers. *Es visible the toma of corriente eléctrica, observándose the generador to the right, and the curiosa matrícula.* (*JMMD*)

A German workshop trailer after a road accident. (*ME*)

Two workshop trailers. Between them is a generator to provide them with electricity. (*JMMD*)

MEDICAL BATTALION (SAN/88) AND CAMPAIGN HOSPITAL (LAZ/88)

The Condor Legion had its own medical battalion, *Sanitäts-Abteilung, San/88*, and each Condor Legion unit had a medical detachment equipped with an ambulance. Various field hospitals were also organized (such as *Lazarett, Laz/88*) and a number of medical establishments were set up at different locations around Nationalist Spain, although they never matched the size of either the Franquist or Italian facilities.

A Horch 830 BL Kfz. 31 next to an Opel Blitz 2-to 3.5 ambulance. (*COT*)

Rear view of a Horch 830 BL ambulance. (*JMMD*)

A number of medical vehicles of the Condor Legion parked outside a hospital in Massalió (Teruel). (*JMMD*)

A Phänomen Granit 25H ambulance. (*JMMD*)

Adler Trumpf Junior Cabriolet belonging to 2.Laz/88. (*JMMD*)

An ambulance on an Opel Blitz 2-to 3.5 chassis. (*JMMD*)

Three-quarter rear view of a Phänomen Granit 25H. (*JMMD*)

Front view of a Kfz. 62 bodied Büssing–NAG G 31 belonging to W/88. (*JMCB*)

METEOROLOGICAL UNIT (W/88)

The Condor Legion had a small meteorological unit, *Wetterstelle, W/88*, which was essential for the proper operation of the Condor Legion air contingent.

The emblem of W/88.